UNIVERSITY
of the
JAZZ
MESSENGERS

Doctoral Dissertation of:

Valery Ponomarev

**ART BLAKEY'S PASSWORDS TO THE
MYSTERY OF CREATING ART AND
UNIVERSAL SUCCESS.**

Advisor, Tutor, and Supervisor
of the Doctoral Program
Abdullah Ibn Buhaina
a.k.a. Art Blakey

BookBaby

7905 N. Crescent Blvd.

Pennsauken, NJ 08110, www.BookBaby.com

Art Blakey's Passwords to the mystery of creating Art and Universal success.

https://vponomarev.com/

ISBN: 978-1-09832-738-5 (print)
ISBN: 978-1-09832-739-2 (ebook)

Snapshot from the Art Blakey video on line.

Can be found here: https://www.youtube.com/watch?v=t5oaiCtckxo.

Walter Davis, David Schnitter, Art Blakey, Valery Ponomarev,
Bobby Watson, Dennis Irwin. Photo by Lev Zabeginski.

Snapshot of Art Blakey from the video Art Blakey and the Jazz Warriors
Pt2. Can be found on YouTube

"I WAS BORN JAMES EDWARD BLAKEY"

- ART BLAKEY.

I heard him say that on many occasions.

Book of Art Blakey Quotes

University of
Art Blakey and the Jazz Messengers

V.M.Ponomarev's Graduation dissertation

"I tell people, 'I was a high School dropout, but I Graduated from
Art Blakey College, the Miles Davis Conservatory of Music and
Charlie Parker University"
(Walter Bishop, Jr. Sent by Peter Zimmerman.)

ACKNOWLEDGMENTS:

I want to thank Dave Brahinsky for his work proof reading this manuscript. Raphael D'Lugoff for looking the book over and making valuable suggestions.

Contents

Illustrations

FOREWORD

I see the need for this book at every gig, whether I play or sit at a club and listen. Every concert, rehearsal, every time I deal with musicians, hear them talk, make announcements, conduct themselves on stage etc. Professional ones, not only students. Brilliant players, but, almost always, lacking the knowledge of the Art Blakey's Teachings. I see it right away.

This book is intended to give the novice who has just embarked on the road of learning to play melodies, scales, chords, fast runs and trills, play in all sorts of bands etc., exposure to many "codes" and "keys" which spell out what is beyond the "obvious", to what he or she will be really dealing with, some for awhile, some will be dealing with it for a long time. Some, all their lives. Once understood, practiced and applied on stage in front of a live audience, these "codes" will serve as an invaluable guiding light. A source of confidence and an inspiration on the way to a close encounter with the mystery of creating Art, playing Music.

The "codes/keys", I am about to reveal, will make a lot of sense to all musicians, but particularly to Jazz Musicians, because they come from Art Blakey himself. One of the greatest personalities in jazz, drummers, band leaders and educators in the history of this music, who in turn learned his craft from the greatest jazz musicians preceding him. Look at these codes as Initiation Rites, Art Blakey & the Jazz Messengers Modus Operandi.

To this day Art Blakey & The Jazz Messengers, one of the most loved and emulated around the world jazz orchestras, is referred to as the most prestigious School of Jazz Music - The Harvard of Jazz Education. How do we know it provided such a high level of education? Well, check out the list of "graduates".

GENEALOGICAL TREE.

Just read these names: ...Clifford Brown, Lee Morgan, Freddie Hubbard, Wynton Marsalis ...

...............Hank Mobley, Benny Golson, Wayne Shorter, Johnny Griffin, Jackie McLean .... Bobby Timmons, Cedar Walton..............

"He worked with Art Blakey" is a mark of distinction of the highest order, a "diploma" associated with anybody who worked with Art Blakey & the Jazz Messengers. Not just sat in once or twice, or played a couple of gigs. No, I mean really worked: rehearsed, performed, traveled, tried his own tunes, recorded, listened to Art talk or observed him at concerts making announcements, emceeing his own concerts, conducting himself on stage, with journalists, club-owners, promoters and agents. It was always a lesson, repeated time after time, just as if it were read out of a text book on different subjects: Stage Manners, How to compose, How to play a solo, How to work on a Ballad etc. etc. on and on, every day for years. From the end of 1976 through 1980 for me full time and almost all the years in the States sitting in, watching the Messengers on stage, hanging with Art.

"WHEN THESE (MUSICIANS) GET TOO OLD, I WILL GET SOME YOUNGER ONES."

(AB, NIGHT AT BIRDLAND)

In Art's words - "This is my thing, to build them up. If the fellow has got it, young man has got it, I believe in putting him out there. We have many, many stars out there who had come through the Messengers" (Art Blakey feat. Freddie Hubbard - Interview & Jodo (F.Hubbard) You Tube)

Like any good teacher, Art knew the value of repetition. Repetition is the key to education. In Russia one can see, or at least in my time at school could have seen, a rhyme posted almost in every class room. Literally translated it would read "Repetition is the Mother of Learning".

When I heard someone being sarcastic about hearing Art say the same thing again, I knew this just did not understand what he was dealing with.

4

Not me. I was lucky to get the idea right away. "Repetition is The Mother Of Learning". That's what it was. So, we, The Messengers, were getting our education.

After all, young people graduate with Bachelors and Masters degrees and enter the work force of America. Then they go through "continuous education" to be able to retain their licenses and to better their qualifications as doctors, bank workers, traders etc. Some even start their professional lives as apprentices and keep on climbing the ladder till they become masters of their profession - managers, executives, movers of industry etc. after digging into all of the nooks and crannies of their profession on the job in banks, factories, hospitals...

The Messengers was that institution, which provided conscripts with the finest in Jazz Education. Quoting Art Blakey -

NO SUBSTITUTE FOR EXPERIENCE.

Why do you think one boxing, tennis, soccer or whatever trainer never, almost never, fails to produce yet another champion and the other, no matter how many times he tries, fails miserably?

Art Blakey and the Jazz Messengers, like a jazz university or conservatory, graduated yet a host of fantastic players, another and yet another one. Of course, one had to have "it" to be admitted to the "University" of Art Blakey and the Jazz Messengers. But once you were in, an incredible wealth of knowledge, accumulated through the years and passed along from generation to generation of musicians playing in bands like Fletcher Henderson, Chick Webb, Earl "Fatha" Hines, Billy Eckstine, Count Basie, Duke Ellington ... **"No substitute for experience"**, was made available to you. Most generously and wisely, with care and respect for the "student". Art Blakey played in most of those bands. Remember the sidemen's names?

Art himself, like so many others - Charlie Parker, Dizzy Gillespie, Miles Davis, Clark Terry, Eddie "Lockjaw" Davis; the list goes on and on - learned from musicians of preceding generations.

There were no jazz schools, there were no jazz courses in universities, there were no any state approved formal jazz education programs anywhere in those times. Just like in the Soviet Union of my time, where formal jazz education was not available, neither in my time nor till well after I left.

I was fortunate to catch and benefit from some of the greatest traditions Jazz generated through the years of it's evolution - learning on the job so to speak, an oral tradition. I still feel privileged and always will.

From the times even before Joe "King" Oliver's Orchestra young musicians learned from older musicians and then passed their experience to the next generations.

"FAIR EXCHANGE IS NO ROBBERY - HAND OUT OUR KNOWLEDGE AND WISDOM TO THE YOUNGER PEOPLE SO THEY CAN TAKE IT FURTHER."

- ART BLAKEY

This is my PhD thesis. I hope you will enjoy reading it. Some of it will be ringing and ringing in your head all by itself, just as if it were being played on some kind of a tape-recorder. Some of it you might want to read and reread. Go ahead, repeat. I had a great time sharing it with you.

Sincerely,

Valery Messenger Ponomarev

Art Blakey & the Jazz Messengers at the 1979 Newport Festival. From Left: Art Blakey, Valery Ponomarev, David Schnitter, Robert Watson, Dennis Irwin. Not pictured: pianist James Williams.

Stage:

"THEY SEE YOU BEFORE THEY HEAR YOU."

There is another one, which fits very well here -

"DON'T TAKE AN AUDIENCE FOR A FOOL (A.B.)"

This postulate, as most of the other ones, I heard from Art Blakey many times. It applies to many situations involving a musician, lecturer, politician, priest etc. on or off the band stand, stage, pulpit, podium, ...whatever. The audience does see you first, not hear you. You come on the band stand, find your spot in front of a microphone, set up a stand for your instrument. (Not a music stand, but that's another subject.) Forget about that one; not in the Messengers. Any ways, you are already under observation. The lesson is - you are always under observation, and influence too. (Another subject, whether you realize it or not.) But we are talking about the stage now.

If you are dressed in rags, sloppy, or God forbid, dirty, people think - what kind of musicians are these? They don't earn enough money to buy decent clothes?

A Jazz artist rarely needs to be dressed in tuxedo. But he does need to be presentable. Slick is fine.

"YOU NEED TO BE COMFORTABLE"

is another Art Blakey quote. He himself very often would spell it out - "Ties make you tight. Buttoned up sports jacket makes you tight and stuffy".

Ties do constrict your breathing - just as my trumpet teacher used to say. You will see it in this book when I spell out the quote **"Don't try to be perfect"**.

Muscle coordination, the importance of being relaxed, all of it is later in this book.

So, one time Art said - "Let's wear overalls". Yeah, work overalls. One would think this kind of an outfit wouldn't look fashionable enough for a high profile orchestra on stage. On the contrary, with a nice shirt and cool shoes, overalls look very good. I do remember Art telling Bobby (Bobby Watson) "Put on your new work clothes and walk up and down 5th Avenue. It'll be a new fashion before you know it."

A couple of days later I happened to be on 5th avenue and 47th Street in New York City looking for a birthday present for my (now long time ex) wife in one of those jewelry shops. And, lo and behold, who do I see? Bobby, dressed up in his best stage clothes walking rather quickly down the most fashionable avenue of NYC. He was trying to look kinda busy, as if he were engrossed in his own thoughts, but he was watching out of the corner of his eye what of an effect he was having on the passers by.

In those years Bobby was slim and tall, just the way a model is supposed to look. The garment looked good on him. He did not see me though. It was very interesting to watch my mate in the Messengers' horn section outside of a musical situation. Before I knew it, Bobby had gotten lost in the crowd.

Guess what? Not much later, lots of people were wearing our overalls. What was originally designed for construction workers, lumberjacks, truck drivers, plumbers and harbor loaders now looked very attractive in singles bars, discotheques, student parties etc. Girls loved those overalls of ours. But as far as comfort, they were unbeatable, better than even a sweat suit. Just look at musicians on the band stand. How restricted a bass-player looks in a suit and tie. The same goes for every band member. A trumpet-player, or any wind instrument player, can't even breathe freely with a tie wrapped around his neck.

For this very reason many other artists gave up the idea of wearing neckties. John Coltrane, for example. How about Clifford Brown, Charlie Parker?

Clifford Brown

Clifford Brown

Charlie Parker

John & Alice Coltrane

Art, Bobby and I.

"It's not what it was designed for. It's what you do with it."

Did you know that the famous ConnConnstellation 38B trumpet was built for a brass band? Not a brass quartet, but a big brass band where the pitch of an individual instrument does not even have to be precise, because it will get lost any way in the multitude of roaring trumpets, trombones, baritone horns, tubas, euphoniums, cymbals, bass and snare drums, the blare of the street or a stadium crowd. A big brass band does not need to be tuned. Did you know that? It's useless.

But jazz musicians loved the ConnConnstellation. From 1956 on, almost every trumpet player you can think of played it: Freddie Hubbard played both the big 5 inch and small 4 inch bells, Lee Morgan also played a 38B model, Maynard Ferguson, Blue Mitchell, Chet Baker - the list goes on and on. Cootie Williams played the ConnConnstellation long cornet model. Regardless of what the instrument had been designed for, it always sounded in tune in the hands of my favorite jazz musicians. I am sure Clifford Brown would've played one, had he not perished in a car crash right before the Connstellation came

14

into fashion. Not Dizzy Gillespie, nor Miles Davis, though. I have never seen them with it. Not live, not in films, not on pictures. Lee Morgan's picture with it on the stage of the infamous Slugs is on the wall of my apartment, along with many other pictures of my Jazz heroes, of course. Jimmy Morgan, Lee Morgan's brother gave it to me. Actually Jimmy's friend Willy gave it to me, but he got it from Lee's brother and then they both decided that I should have it.

Lee Morgan at Slugs the week of February 19, 1972 with Freddie Waits, Billy Harper, Reggie Workman & Harold Mabern

Going back to overalls. Let's call them " The ConnConnstellation" of Jazz Tux. Most of mine I gave away to girls. But one pair is still in my closet for shirts, jackets and slacks. They were very loose on me once and very comfortable. Now I need to shed some pounds to be able to wear them, but they are there. One day I may surprise you.

They see you before they hear you goes further than that.

NEVER ASK IN FRONT
OF THE AUDIENCE
"WHAT DO WE PLAY NEXT?"

"What is this song?" "How does that one go?" or "What key?" Never teach the music in front of the audience. At a jam session you can, but not at a concert with a high profile band.

To the audience it means you don't know what you are doing.

In Art's words - "People make an event out of it, they pay for tickets, sometimes very expensive ones, they dress up for it, come to the club or a concert hall full of expectations and see guys on the bandstand who don't even know what to play or who start a big discussion on what to play for a feature, what changes for the tune they want to use". It looks totally stupid. The first thing coming to the listener's mind is "I thought I was going to experience a performance of the highest artistic level. I paid my money for this? They don't even know what to play." That's utter disappointment right there.

Musicians should know their repertoire before stepping on the band stand. Not any kind of a crib on the stage either. Uh, uh! Benny Golson once told me a story of the Messengers sitting in a circle and memorizing the tunes. They actually collectively practiced memorizing their repertoire. I heard that story years after leaving the band but always knew that Art Blakey did not invent that "stage rule" just for our generation of the Messengers. Benny Golson was talking about Lee Morgan, Bobbie Timmons, Jymie Merritt, the classic addition of the band, my heroes, before recording in 1958 one of the greatest Jazz Albums ever - Moanin'.

The Messengers had never even had music stands on the stage. The band projected confidence. People were happy to have paid whatever money they paid for the show. They were put in the right state of mind from the very beginning.

On the stage we had never discussed what an opener or the following tune was going to be. Art just played an intro and from his drumming we would know which song was coming. Whether it was Jody, Uranus or Gipsy Folk Tales, each is in the exact tempo set by the opening drum figured piece. For your feature he would make the most generous announcement and tell the audience: **"He has chosen for his musical vehicle"** then followed the title of a tune Art knew would feature you the most.

To stop playing and give directions to the sound engineer from the stage was totally unacceptable. No matter how wrong, almost all of the time, the "nasty guy" in the sound booth could've been, none of us would ever stop playing and indicate it in front of an audience. Some times during the break or after the concert we would've given hell to the culprit, but not during the performance. From the stage? Oh, no.

I never heard Art giving instructions nor advice in front of the audience. Only "off the record". Every one of us heard Art's **"It's your feature"** meaning, when its your turn to be center stage, be that center of attention. Don't give extra time for the piano or other instrument to play as long or longer than you. **"They will have their turn. Don't confuse the listener."** Give the piano trio or the bass 8, OK 16 bars, and that's it. Come back and finish your presentation.

"DON'T LOOK UNHAPPY ON THE BANDSTAND."

(A.B.)

Tired, uninterested, or, God forbid, yawning, etc.

I was guilty of it a lot. Chops are down, a bad sounding room or poor acoustics in general produce a very negative effect. Everybody, particularly brass and wind instrument players, has to over blow and as a result lose their chops. You feel unhappy and it shows. To the audience it looks bad. The audience does not know that the sound engineer did his lousy trick yet again. They think you don't like what you are doing. What is the point of playing then? If you don't like what you are playing, how do you expect the audience to like it. The same goes for writing music. You put on paper what you really like, what awakens strong emotion, which goes with the idea for the song. You like it? Believe me, the listener will like it too.

Oh, no, don't look unhappy on the band stand, no matter what! Sometimes a musician is concerned with problems which have nothing to do with music.

Leave everything behind before you step onto the band stand. Everything! "He is worried about his girlfriend back in New York." I heard Art saying it many times and it always sounded sarcastic or even like an accusation. As if he wanted to say "What? You are on a tour with the Messengers and your mind is absorbed by a girl some six thousand miles away, who is scolding you for not taking her to Rome, Berlin, London or Madrid with you? Yeah, yeah, and spending all that money on her?"

"WHEN PLAYING MUSIC THINK OF MUSIC. NOTHING IS MORE IMPORTANT THAN THAT AT THE MOMENT."

When hearing for the first time almost every postulate of Art's I always felt like I knew it already. It made so much sense. But who knows if I would've had the same attitude had I never heard Art saying this or another postulate. Or heard it from somebody else, not Art. When you are driving, what do you think about, or at least should? Driving, right? What happens when you take your mind off your driving? Missed exits, wrong roads, empty gas tank, or, god forbid, even worse. Don't want even to talk about it.

The same with music. How could you possibly take your mind off it when actually performing? You know what will happen: wrong chords, messed up forms, lost precision, sloppy entrances, wrong lanes, fatal accidents. Oh. no, please!............

When you are done with your solo, the music still goes on. Take a bow and move backwards, still facing the audience. Do not turn your back on the fans. You wouldn't like it, would you? So, they wouldn't either. Yes, I know what you are going to tell me - How about Miles Davis turning his back to the audience? Yes, that's true, Miles Davis is known for that. But that's an exception to the rule. He is known for breaking rules, too. I don't think there has ever been a rule without an exception.

Anyway, do not turn your back to the audience. That's it. Do not turn your back to your band mates either, do not stand in front of a soloist. Oh, please! Don't do that. Remain on the stage, though. Find yourself a comfortable spot and remain there. The music still goes on. Concentrate on that. Listen to what the others are playing. You cannot look indifferent. You are a part of it, even if you are not playing at the moment.

I very often see young players looking scornful and even grimacing while other band members are playing. Have you ever been guilty of it? You want to send a message to the audience that you are better and more important than the others? Be reasonable! You are in the same band. The other guys have to be as good as you are, or better. Or you are all bad. To exclaim during the concert - "That was a wrong chord!" or "You read that bar wrong!" No!

"Tune your instrument. You are out of tune." No! Read my lips - Not during a performance, not in front of an audience. You can bring it up after the show is over, if there was really something wrong. Not on stage! You got it? Thank you!

Do not clean nor fix your instrument in front of the audience. If something broke, that's probably the only time when you can leave the stage, so you can fix it without anybody in the auditorium knowing it. General rule - whatever goes wrong, and it does more often than it should - a musical "atom bomb" goes off - you smile and keep on listening and admiring the music like nothing happened. Keep this in mind: you and the rest of the band know what arrangement you prepared for this particular concert. Listeners don't. Jazz, for the most part, is improvised music. What comes out spontaneously might be much better than what had been planned. And very often it is. Unplanned endings, cues, chords, lines, titles, names etc. in any form of arts, sports, or speeches, you name it, are legendary.

Sonny Rollins, Clifford Brown and scores of other musicians were unhappy about their solos after recording sessions. The same very recordings proved to be masterpieces later.

"DO NOT LOOK AT YOUR WATCH WHILE ON STAGE."

(A.B.)

Yes, I've heard A.B. saying that more than once. It means - If you are looking at your watch during the concert, you are sending a message that music is not your prime interest at the moment. Whatever it might be, it's not music. How could that be? Art Blakey himself would ask what time it was. He himself did forget about everything else while playing, time included. But he was the leader of the band and it was his responsibility to stop the band and go on break so, the club's management could change the audience for the next set or bring the concert to an end according to the club's rules or even Local Unions regulations sometimes etc. It was not the band's responsibility. We were free to lose track of time and blow our hearts out. We did.

Too many don'ts? Well, this is the stage we are talking about. The Stage is sacred ground. A Place of magic. The Stage has its laws, which need to be learned and strictly observed. Don't you remember the first time you stepped on it? I certainly do, very well. I thought I'd lose my footing. My knees were shaking, my mind was blurred and wondering around, time stopped, I was practically floating in another zone and messed up a song I knew very well. Yes, that other dimension opened up and engulfed me. I was in the land of Enchantment. It wasn't the famous "stage fright" either, or better, "audience fright." No. Because there wasn't any audience. Just a couple of pioneers (in Russia of my time almost all kids belonged to the Pioneer Association) hanging around. Been on the Stage for the first time, that's what it was. I will always remember it.

"DID YOU WANNA BE A MUSICIAN?"

One of Art's sayings was meant to really ask you - are you ready to cope with all the drawbacks and shortcomings of the musical profession, particularly Jazz ? How important is playing music to you? Once on the stage, you forget about all of that. You are playing music. That's the reward and the blessing already. Getting to the stage is the job. Better get used to it.

Once we were real close to Russia. Just thinking of it brings out in perfect detail that now very distant moment…

The band had just flown from New York to Helsinki, Finland. First stop – the Pori Jazz Festival, a rather long ride from the airport. No time for the hotel. We went directly to the concert location instead... I was standing under the tent, which separated me from the pouring rain, and chewing, between warm-ups, on a stale sandwich.

Russia was so near, yet it was out of reach behind the Iron Curtain. That's when Art's husky voice startled me with: "Did you wanna be a musician, Valery?"

Walter Davis, David Schnitter, Valery Ponomarev, Dennis Irwin, Bobby Watson and Art Blakey.............

He thought I was lost in thoughts in my mind going over crazy schedules, life on the road, dealing with agents, different time zones, being away from home/family, etc. No, he was wrong this time. I was thinking of St. Petersburg, which was only a bus ride from where we were, but it was not very likely I could take that ride any time soon. It turned out to be 17 years before I could return to Russia for the first time.

But those or any other drawbacks of the music profession never distracted me. Music, that's all that mattered. To get to the stage, to play with Art Blakey, that's what mattered first and foremost. And it was the same for all of my brothers in the Messengers.

"PLAYING MUSIC IS NOT A JOB FOR ME. I JUST ENJOY IT. GETTING TO THE CONCERT IS A JOB."

(A.B)

(Al Bright - Art Blakey Post Performance Interview - 1980 You Tube) **"You don't quit what you love. Playing music is my life. When they pat me in the face with a feather, then I quit."**

Didn't I hear that enough times? Playing with Art Blakey and the Jazz Messengers was like being in Musical Heaven. There is no way anybody can look at being in Heaven as a job, work or labor. Bobby and I discussed this idea more than once while driving for many hours from gig to gig when flying was not an option. Actually, driving was fun too. For the most part anyway.

Once we were driving a long time and it was getting late. Art "O.D.ed" on driving (an extremely rare occasion) and was snoozing in the back seat. Bobby and I were exchanging driving duties. James Williams, after almost driving us all into a ditch, stopped driving. Bobby, of course, was trying to outdo me and was speeding in the 55 mph zone up to 80. All of a sudden, a voice too familiar to all of us said "You are too fast Bobby, you are driving above 80." "I thought you said drive 80." My brother in the Messengers said trying to get out of the "guilty" zone. "I said take 80, route 80, not drive 80 miles an hour in a 55 mph zone."

For the most part, the road schedule of the Messengers could be safely carved in stone: First take the earliest plane to what could be anywhere in the world, check into a hotel, shower, meet half an hour later in the lobby to go to the concert location for the sound check.

While the microphones, wires, speakers and monitors were being set up, you warmed up. After telling the sound engineer enough times "once you establish the volume, don't change anything," the sound check is considered over and everybody heads to a restaurant to grab something to eat before the gig. In some variations of the schedule there were sandwiches served after the sound check.

It had happened more than once that we would get stuck somewhere on our travels and arrive at the location right before the audience started filling up the place, or even when the audience was already waiting. In that case you would get on the bandstand and play, skipping all of the preliminary steps except warming up.

After the concert, there was a dinner organized by the promoter with all of his friends, sponsors and friends of sponsors invited. Going to bed early almost never happened. If there was any jazz club within driving distance, we headed there to hang out, returning to the hotel in time to pack, maybe sleep for a couple of hours and then drive to the next gig or head to the airport early in the morning to catch the first plane out. It could be to a place we had just come from the day before, like when we made it from Palermo to Paris and then right back to the South of Italy the very next day, to repeat the same travel-arrival-hotel-sound-check-concert-dinner-hang-hotel sequence again.

That schedule would repeat and repeat until the string of one night-ers was broken and we would find ourselves in London for a two week run at "Ronnie Scott's." Or at "Domicile" on Leopold Strasse in Munich for a Thursday through Sunday engagement. Or any of the world's capitals for two days to a week. Even being in New York didn't feel like being at home, but rather in a city on the itinerary. Or we simply got stuck in the middle of nowhere in a hotel for a day off. Japan, Europe, or the States – it didn't matter. The Sisyphean labors would go on unchallenged 52 weeks out of a year.

"APPLAUSE - IS FOOD FOR THE ENTERTAINER!"

Oh yeah, that one.

Always thank the audience for showing you its appreciation of your performance. In whatever form it may come: applause, hand clapping, feet tapping, whistling, head shaking, screaming, yelling, etc.

Different bands and musicians had their own ways of showing appreciation. Dexter Gordon, for example, would extend his hands to the audience holding his saxophone in them, but not bow. We took bows, individually after playing solos or collectively after the concert and all the encores were over.

At one of the first concerts with the Messengers after my feature I took a bow to the audience and then to Art, who was standing in front of the band and also applauding me. Of course I knew it was a part of the show, but it was incredibly flattering nevertheless. I kept bowing with my trumpet in my left hand and my right hand on the left part of my chest. I never took any kind of "course" on how to bow, never read any books on gestures up until then. I had just known since childhood that artists bow after their performances.

Art loved it, I knew it because he mimicked my gesture, and bowed back to me, making sure he bowed deeper than I. So, of course, I had to outdo him and so on. So we've ended up bowing to each other like a couple of Japanese guys as I've seen so many times on every trip to Japan afterwards. Boy, didn't the audience love it!

What is it, a Russian bowing or something? Art asked me right away. No, I said, I just bowed. Of course he knew that the right hand on the left side of the chest means "From the heart". You really mean it. From that point on this bowing thing became a fixture, a part of the show. After every feature of mine Art and I would go into our act, trying to out bow each other to the delight of every audience. Except I would always bow to Art first. He was my audience too.

"THEY ARE STILL APPLAUDING" -

when you heard Art Blakey's voice saying it after the last note of the concert had stopped reverberating and you and your instrument were already off the stage, it almost sounded like a command - we go back and play an encore. Always. Even if we were late for a plane or tired from severe lack of sleep you go back on the stage and play an encore. Don't you ever turn your back on the audience. Oh, no, never.

"THEY ARE APPLAUDING BECAUSE THEY ARE HAPPY YOU FINISHED"

AB would say it after someone would lose track of time and immerse himself in an endless repetition of chorus after chorus, forgetting about everything and everybody. Particularly, forgetting about "Music as a Collective Product" and just staying on an orbit of his own. Easy to understand, considering that Art always provided such incredible accompaniment. Always! Applause coming from the audience would launch the soloist, already lost in musical space, further into the vastness of the audio expanse. Sometimes applause would burst out for a reason totally unrelated to the music, like a window being opened or closed, more people flocking into the over packed house, or fans standing up and leaving to provide room for those waiting in agony outside. But the guy "in orbit" wouldn't know any of that and would let the sound of applause catapult him further and further away from the concert, audience, the stage, the other horn players, "music as a collective product" and would keep on blowing his brains out. Just like an athlete losing the self-preservation instinct during a highly intense competition.

I've heard, more than once, that such incidents sometimes turn tragic and end up in the athlete falling dead in the middle of a soccer field, ski track, or marathon race... The inertia of competing takes them there. Music and sports again. That's when Art's "They're applauding because they thought you finished " would bring the "space traveler" safely back to earth. Art had a perfect comment for any and every situation it seemed.

"DON'T TRY TO BE PERFECT. IF YOU MADE A MISTAKE, MAKE IT LOUD, MAKE MUSIC OUT OF IT."

Didn't I hear that enough times? Oh, yes, I did. Addressed to me directly. And still being very visibly upset at every "cockroach" of a mistake creeping in my playing. It did take me a minute to realize that after all what had come out unintended was not necessarily bad. It was just not what I intended to play, that's all. So many times I had been unhappy with my recordings. But listening to them months or even years later made me think: "That's not that bad". There are many "mistakes" on legendary recordings. How about So Near So Far played by Miles Davis. There is a little roll in brushes at the very end of the head out. It came out accidentally. So what? Sounds beautiful. "Don't try to be perfect". I am sure there are many more recorded examples. If you know of one/ones, please send them to me. I'd be happy to include them in the next addition of this thesis. I will mention your name too.

The same with playing. The listener does not know what you planned, he hears what came out. Do not deny him the right to his own judgment. He may like what came out. But if you grimace as if some mosquito bit you, then there is no chance. It's just like telling somebody: you are dumb, stupid, deaf, you don't deserve to belong to a concert going community. You keep on doing that and the guy in the audience will ask for his money back, figuratively speaking.

Trying to be perfect makes one restricted and uptight. One can not make music in this condition. Relax. Playing an instrument, any instrument, requires muscle coordination. (I've heard that there is one musical instrument which does not, but for the life of me I can't imagine which one that is. With so many instruments out there and just one not fitting into general rule? Well, there are always exceptions to the rules. Almost everyone. Almost every rule has been broken too. "Don't try to be perfect" again?)

The best players always have excellent muscle coordination. Just like athletes. For that reason most musicians are very good at sports. I have never actually met a good musician who was not good at sports. At least one kind of sports. Miles Davis was an excellent boxer, Art Blakey practiced boxing with his son Gamal. I was at those sessions more than once. Lee Morgan and Art Blakey practiced Karate (Illustration). Lee Morgan was also a very good basketball player. Freddie Hubbard was an excellent pool player. He could've been good at other sports too, I just have never heard about it..........

And the other way around. I have seen Muhammad Ali on a television show singing, and Roberto Duran playing percussion instruments. Did somebody say Reggie Miller plays an instrument? He collects jazz for sure.

So says Michael Scott of NBC's *The Office*—and he's not wrong! The comparison has been made by everyone from basketball Hall of Famer Kareem Abdul-Jabbar (I grew up loving Jazz. Listens to Jazz since the age of 7 years old. Duke Ellington, Count Basie, Sonny Rollins, John Coltrane - Some of the people I admired. Their music went through my head when I was playing. Q- Would you have wonted to trade places with Coltrane, Monk A- Oh, yeah, definitely. I wish I could've played bass) to Jazz at Lincoln Center's own Wynton Marsalis.

For athletes it is so important to be relaxed. If you are uptight - you lose the fight, literally. The same for musicians. One of my trumpet teachers used to say relax, relax. Then he would tighten his neck and throat muscles and with a very raspy voice say: "When the muscles are tight I can't even talk, how could I play trumpet." And then he would loosen his neck and with a very good clear voice continue the instruction. There are exercises for relaxing the shoulder, neck and throat muscles which are widely used by vocalists and all wind instruments players. They are used by lecturers, public speakers, actors, priests, announcers too. The same very ones. Relax, don't try to be perfect.

Woody Show practiced Tai-Chi a lot. There is a picture of him on the Internet, taken before the show at the legendary Key Stone Corner in San Francisco. Also his album Master Of The Art on the Electra/Musician label features Shaw's photo by Carol Friedman practicing Tai-Chi

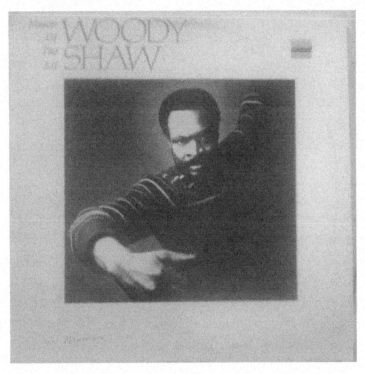

Woody Shaw practicing Tai chi

I have seeing him doing all sorts of "katas" before many a concert.

Drummer-Boxer Stan Levey

Stan Levey, one of the strongest drummers of his generation, He played in Philly with Dizzy Gillespie's group in 1942, at the age of 16. Involved in the formative years of bebop and accepted as one of bop's most important drummers. In New York he and Dizzy worked on 52nd Street with Charlie Parker and Oscar Pettiford. Stan has played on over 2000 recordings. He has performed with most of the greatest names in the music business. People such as:Dizzy Gillespie, Charlie Parker, Coleman Hawkins, Art Tatum, Ben Webster, Scott LaFaro, Victor Feldman, Dexter Gordon, Errol Garner, Miles Davis, George Shearing, Lester Young, Roy Eldrige, Thelonius Monk, Hank Jones, Oscar Peterson, and many more...

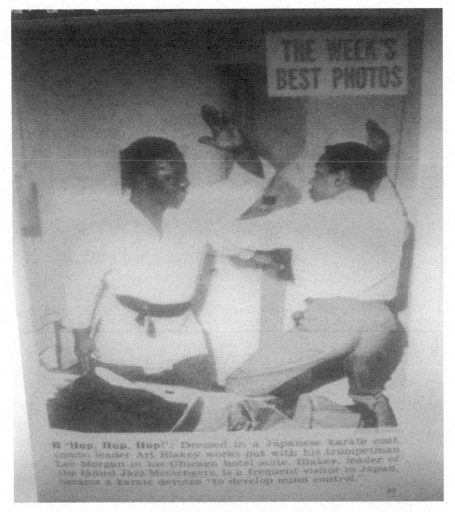

AB and Lee Morgan practicing Tai Chi

"Everybody has an idol. Mine (A.B.'s) were Chick Webb (used to valet for him. AB), Sid Catlett, Kenny Clarke is my biggest influence" (He had taught Art).

"You don't make a god (idol) out of a human being." I'm trying to teach that to all of my musicians. I believe in this music because it's the truth. (Truth is stranger than fiction!)

I could not understand it at first. Because my idol was Clifford Brown. His playing was so perfect, so beautiful, so exciting and wise. Why couldn't I always try to be like that. But Art did repeat this statement more than once, not necessarily addressing me, but definitely making sure that I was within ear shot. Hm, what was he saying?

At the club Concerts by the Sea, on the new edition of the Messengers' first trip to California, Freddie Hubbard came to the club. One of my trumpet heroes, of course. Art featured me on a ballad of my own choice, which was "Autumn in New York" at the time.

On the break, Freddie engaged me in a conversation. I felt kinda awkward. The number 1 trumpet player in the world just asked me about my diet. I did not know much about diets at the time and said "I eat anything".

"Oh, you are on a see food diet. You eat whatever you see".

Oh, yes. That's it I was happy to confirm. Now I felt more comfortable to tell this giant of modern jazz that I had always loved his playing and transcribed very many of his solos.

"Clifford is your man. But thank you anyway. You need to find your own voice, work on your own style."

That was it. That's what Art was trying to teach me. Jesus! Did he tell that to Freddie at one time too? Who knows? After all Freddie Hubbard was a very young man when he first joined the Messengers. Clifford was his idol at one time too, by his own admission. Lee Morgan's also. How do you like that?

Oh, my! Did Clifford hear the same "lectures"? How do you like that?

I knew by then that Dizzy Gillespie as a young man wanted to play like Roy Eldridge, Clifford Brown like Harry "Sweets" Edison and then Fats Navarro. On his early recordings Clifford Brown sounds just like him. Wayne Shorter wanted to play like Lester Young, Oscar Peterson wanted to sound like Nat King Cole, Sonny Rollins like Coleman Hawkins and the list goes on and on....

And then what? No matter how hard you try, there is no way you can become somebody else. Every one has his/her own voice. It's like fingerprints. They are unique and belong to only one individual. To copy and study a master's playing, acting, dancing, sporting moves, you name it, is an extremely useful tool. Speaking of music, Jazz in particular, one learns articulation, how to play staccato or legato, to syncopate, play in time etc. from the best possible source. So try with all your might to get as close to your idol as possible. Don't worry about sounding like that musical giant or another one. You can't become somebody else. But you will learn to "speak" properly. Then your own "fingerprints" will start to show, more and more if you keep on working at it.

Finding my own style. That's what it was. Sure enough I started practicing different melodic lines, mixing up pentatonic scales and apply them to the tunes we were playing. I thought nobody would ever notice it.

"Valery is working on his new style" a week or so later I heard Art saying to no one in particular. Just making sure that the sound of the words was in earshot. Only then I remembered that his room turned out to be next to mine in one of the hotels we stayed at. So, he must've heard me practicing. Art did not miss much if it had to do at least somewhat with his band. What a better confirmation did one need than "Yes, Val, you did get the point."

I first met the "Greatest", not long after moving to the US, at Boomers, the legendary New York jazz club on Bleecker Street, now defunct, but still a legend. All the best Jazz musicians used to hang out there. Junior Cook, David Schnitter, Slide Hampton, Woody Shaw, Harold Mabern, Cedar Walton, Billy Higgins, you name it, whoever happened to be in the city at the time. Art Blakey was a regular at Boomers. One day Bob Cooper, the club owner, invited me to meet Freddie Hubbard.

"Freddie Hubbard is at the club?"

The number 1 jazz trumpet player in the World, according to all the Jazz Magazines and Critics Polls, and one of my trumpet heroes, was sitting at the end of the bar and nursing a drink just like a regular customer.

"I'm in town for a couple of days for a recording. I hear you like Clifford Brown."

33

"Yes, I've transcribed almost every one of his solos available."

"Me too. Love his playing"

Just for the record, Lee Morgan had studied Clifford's playing too and, starting at age 13, took several lessons with him. It is obvious, particularly judging from Lee's earlier recordings. *Donald Byrd*, Lee Morgan, Booker Little, Arturo Sandoval, Freddie Hubbard, Wynton Marsalis, Tom Harrell, you name it, almost every trumpet-player studied Clifford's recordings. Donald Byrd on some albums sounds just like a Clifford Brown clone.

Learning from one's predecessors. In those times everybody did. Here we go again.

"GIVE CREDIT WHERE IT'S DUE."

Another jewel from The Master.

We always learn from somebody. Books - somebody wrote them, Music - somebody played it and/or composed it, the oral tradition - That's a lot of "Somebody's" out there. Whether it came from the universally acknowledged masters of the past, contemporary artists, or even your own students or just a novice. Or a child. You have heard the sayings "a Child Speaks The Truth", Children and fools speak the truth, Children and babies speak the truth. We learn most often from the environment around us not even noticing how our subconscious gets filled up. We never have a problem saying "I learned this from a book by this and that author in school. I learned that from a transcription of the solo/solos played by my favorite trumpet player, saxophone player etc." and you proudly give a name of a musical giant. But very often it's not as easy or natural to a lot of people to name an "unexpected" source. Ah, ah, that is not fair, not honest, not noble.

If you learned something from some body, acknowledge it, thank him/her for that. That will be your friend for life. Imitation is the highest form of flattery. Do not pretend you had known that already, that you did not need to hear it from this particular person. Besides losing a friend, you will not get anything useful out of this source ever again. You will never even know how many times this person had a chance to recommend you to somebody, turn a gig your way, warn you of impending trouble or just show you something very useful as an instrumentalist that could have shown you some "little" trick, which for some reason had been eluding you for years, keeping a door to range, sound, endurance, sight-reading etc. shut to you.

Every great jazz musician imitated somebody before him. Every one learned their solos, styles, even mannerism and speech. Learned, studied and practiced some times for years before coming up with a style of their own. Or, I'd rather say, arriving at a point where their personalities took over. I have heard Wayne Shorter, and many other people, speaking in Art Blakey's voice. Dennis Irwin used to entertain us all speaking in Art's voice. Human speech is music too. You know that, right?

I have heard of Freddie Hubbard complaining to other trumpet-players about copying his lines. I think it's only natural to learn from such a giant. Even if someone wanted to hide the source, no one could. It's too obvious. I hear other players quoting Freddie all the time.

And, of course, one can learn from anywhere and anybody. But I had never expected some one to follow me with a tape recorder. Particularly such a good trumpet-player (name withheld) . I did see him sitting around, just like any other musician hanging out at a club.

One day I was in my practice room doing something, not practicing. Otherwise I would've turned off the radio in the living room and all of a sudden hear "myself" on WBGO playing. I went to the living room and realized somebody else was playing a line I developed years ago out of Clifford Brown's phrase. Then the announcement came and it turned to be the new recording of the guy at the club. Wow, that's a great compliment. When I saw that guy again I told him that I heard his new recording and liked it very much, particularly the part where he used my line. The "culprit" in question got upset and left. Mad with me! Wait a second. What did I do? It took him a year or so to come up to me and say, with great difficulty, thank you for the line. That was many years ago and I had never seen him again. Too bad I did not have a chance to share with him at least a little bit of Art Blakey's wisdom.

One time in Paris Art said - "Come with me to the club where Kenny Clarke is playing. He was my teacher." (The name of the club escapes me).

"Oh, wow!" I had heard of many American Jazz musicians moving to Europe because of economics, playing opportunities and even racial problems. Johnny Griffin, Dexter Gordon, Idrees Sulieman, Carmell Jones, ... and Kenny Clarke. Can't wait to hear him play live and meet him.

There he was. An old man, short and small in stature. He was this person who taught Art Blakey to set up drums and cymbals, hold sticks, hit the snare drum, tom-tom and bass drum, who gave him practicing routines, showed him how play press roll, coordinate hands, arms, legs and feet. He is the one who taught Art Blakey. The leader of the Jazz Messengers!!!

Art Blakey was all ears, looking at his musical life line provider most respectfully. Not adding anything, just listening. I wonder if time played a trick on Art and sent him back to some 40 years previous, when today's Jazz Giant was a young man and had just started to discover the magic of making music.

The aging professor was reciting stories from the past, laughing at his own recollections and holding the center attention. (Usually Art Blakey's part.) Art did not interfere at all. He looked like a very respectful student. It had to be the trick of time. Art was in a zone, another dimension where he was getting his education.

"That is my teacher. My teacher."

It sounded as an old Russian woman in some distant Siberian village talking to even older woman from the same or neighboring village. She would always call her "nanny". The men have similar tradition, according to which the younger generation call their predecessor "Teacher". **Give**

credit where it's due. I heard Art Blakey saying that many times. All doors open for a thankful heart.

LYRICS.

By the time I came to America I was already very aware of the importance of the lyrics to songs. By then I had heard that Ray Charles, for example, loved American Standards first for their lyrics and then for the melodies. I have heard that the words to the song hold the melody together and help the performer to convey the meaning of the song even if he or she is not singing it, but playing it on an instrument. I thought it was obvious and even knew lyrics to a couple of songs like "What's New". First I learned them because it helped me to study English. Listening to the words and repeating them was my thing. Just like studying the solos of my favorite musicians.

Obvious or not, but sometimes musicians, even vocalists, don't pay attention to the lyrics they sing.

Maria Kelly always comes to my mind, an Italian singer, who traveled with an Italian jazz orchestra I worked with every summer for many years after graduating from Art Blakey & the Jazz Messengers. She could really sing. Any Italian would've been proud of her beautiful voice, range, dynamics, articulation -you name it. From the very first sounds of whatever song she would sing it was obvious that this young lady had come out of an incredible vocal tradition. Whether it was a Neapolitan song or an American standard. She did not speak a word of English though, none, but articulated the syllables of English words as clearly as an American girl would've done. Many an American tourist after presenting her with a bouquet of flowers and complimenting on beautiful performance would find out, to their chagrin, that she did not understand a word of their greetings and switch to a broken Italian. What, ley no parlare Englese?

Massimo Mariconi, the bass-player on some of the gigs, who spoke very good English, and I used to laugh our hearts out, after the show and away from the stage of course, recollecting the delivery of Lady Is A Tramp, When The Saints Go Marching In, Body And Soul, or whatever the songs it could've been, with exactly the same passion and emotional charge. No deviation whatsoever. I don't think Maria had ever heard Ella Fitzgerald or Dinah Washington either.

Well, it was Italy during the height of a tourist season, blue skies, the Mediterranean, the Apennine Peninsular, crowds of carefree vacationers everywhere, packed bars, restaurants, gelaterias (Ice cream parlors), spiaggias (beaches), of course, dance floors, discotheques, at every hotel. Sing Maria, sing! We had fun. How could you not? But lyrics do matter!

Future Messenger, Valery Ponomarev, 6 years of age at the summer camp in Karalovo, a hamlet near Moscow. Front row, first on the right.

People told me I had good voice, but I never thought it was something special. It kinda came with my person. Since I was very little I had heard the stories, mainly from my mother, that her mother, my grand mother, was a classically trained singer and a featured soloist at the Moscow Cathedral of Christ the Savior Choir, one of the best in Russia before the revolution 1917.

Anyway, I liked playing ballads and knew quite a few of them. They are actually beautiful American songs turned Jazz standards and just like Ray Charles said, lyrics are more important to the songs than the melody itself. A couple of times I even sung "What's New" to the utter delight of my friends Igor and Irene's mother who had a gathering on the occasion of getting an open telephone line with Israel, where Igor and Irene had recently moved.

The first time I sat in with Art Blakey, I played "The Theme" and then "What's New." I figured he liked my rendition of it because after the concert the God of Drums said and repeated, "You will be playing with my band, you will be playing with my band".

When I finally joined the Messengers two years later, Art featured me on a ballad at every concert, sometimes twice a concert. This took place in Brazil then in Europe. The scene repeated itself again and again at every concert location. I knew he liked my treatments of ballads. He even said so, not only featuring me almost every concert but saying "When Valery plays a ballad, girls long for love". That's the way he put it. I took it as a very high compliment, of course.

So it was at Copenhagen's Montmartre that everything repeated itself as if in a movie which you loved the first time and watched it again and again. There was a packed house, Art's many friends, excited people and tons of applause. In the second set for my feature I played "Blue Moon", at Art's request, and got a storm of applause for it.

After the set Art was relaxing at the table with his many friends when I passed by, feeling proud of myself. A sound of a very familiar harsh voice stopped me in my tracks. "You need to learn the lyrics to the ballad you're playing," I heard Art saying from the table. I came closer.

"WHEN YOU WORK ON A BALLAD, YOU NEED TO LEARN NOT ONLY THE MELODY AND CHANGES, BUT THE LYRICS TOO,

because when people listen to your performance of their favorite song, they recognize right away whether you do or you don't know what you are playing about. At least familiarize yourself with the words, so you know the general mood of the tune". (I was familiar with the lyrics to all the ballads I played, but knew and sang only a couple)

I heard Art telling that to David and Bobby, when they tried a new ballad for their feature number, but he never said anything to me about this.

"Sit down," Art invited me. "You see Valery, you have a beautiful tone, and you feel the tune so well, but you still need to learn the lyrics." And he went on with the whole lecture, which I listened at full attention, knowing that Art had heard something wrong in my rendition of the famous standard. He taught us many things, verbally and by his actions, and he always knew what he was talking about.

I had something on my mind when I asked him, "Is it only the horn players who need to know the lyrics, or the rhythm section players too?"

"Of course, everyone should know them," was the answer.

Art had never become just one of the guys for me. As long as I knew him, he remained a living legend and my hero.

"Art," I began, "we are in Denmark. Where will I find the lyrics now? Please write them out for me"

The atmosphere around us tensed right away. Everybody was looking at me with a serious question in their eyes, as if they were asking: "Are you sure you did the right thing, putting the great superstar on the spot?"

It seemed to me that even Art looked at me with sparkles of annoyance in his eyes. Without saying anything to me, he called the club-owner and asked for a pen and a piece of paper, which appeared right away like out of thin air. Art, not even looking at me, just spread the sheet of paper with the club's stationary on the table and got down to working. The pen didn't look very comfortable between his fingers, which were used to drumsticks, but he was moving it in a slow and steady rhythm without any deviation. Like if it were some kind of a mechanical hand. He kept moving it and moving it, then turned the sheet around and kept on writing. I thought I saw that funny look in his eyes again when he handed me the paper.

"It will help you to play the song like you know it," he growled.

"Art," I said, "please sign it for me: "For Valery to play better, or something" He broke into the big smile of a flattered man. "Come on Valery, you are kidding. You are a Messenger yourself. You don't need my autograph."

Blue Moon

You saw me standing alone
Whithout a dream in my Heart
Whithout a love of my own
Blue Moon you knew just what
I was there for

You heard me saying a prayer
for
Some one I really could care
for
And then there suddenly
appeared before me
The only one my arms could
ever hold
(only)

43

Autograph

He kept on smiling as he was signing: "Written for Valorie by Art Blakey."

His daughter Evelyn for years used to call me Valory instead of Valery.

My first couple of months with the Messengers I tried a different ballad every concert: "My One and Only Love", "Stars Fell On Alabama", "Once In A While", "Autumn in New York", "April in Paris", "Willow Weep For Me" and

44

other ones. Art just made his usual announcement and left it up to me what ballad to play. But he put a stop to it after I played "I Remember Clifford" for the first time. From that point on I ended up playing it each and every feature of mine. AB would just announce it after going through his usual presentation of a featured artist.

Some months later I did try, for the one and only time, a different ballad, Nature Boy - Art took it for granted that I would play what I had been playing every night and stopped short of announcing it. This was at the Rising Sun. It was located on Cherbourg Street in Montreal. That's where Arturo Sandoval and Paquito D'Rivera were in the audience, when they left Cuba for the first time. To be precise, they were not in the audience, but stood in the doorway and clapped their hearts out with the packed club after I finished my feature. That was probably the most intense applause I had ever had up till then.

"I loved the way you played it Val" said the tuba player Ray Draper, who was traveling with us at the moment, as the club's patrons were still turning their applause into a storm.

Art had never told me, nor asked me what tune I would play. Either he waited for me to start or, after I went through many a ballad, would announce "I Remember Clifford".

The very next evening at Rising Sun, after going through his usual presentation of a featured artist, Art Blakey, in a distinctively stern voice, asked me what ballad I was going to play. His voice was so stern, that it did not leave any doubt as per what to play. Or, I'd rather say, what not to play. Whatever I was going to present, it shouldn't have been Nature Boy; I realized that right away. **"I Remember Clifford"** I said, trying to figure out what went wrong the night before.

Don't get me wrong. That is one of the very few compositions, which I can play every day and never feel even remotely bored, but rather feel as if I had heard it for the first time, it feels as if a thick cloud of beautiful memory, terrible loss, wisdom, goodness, kindness and the inevitable had enveloped everything. Does that mean that Benny Golson's creation is a "Perfect Melody"?

I have heard that scientists, through many experiments, have proved beyond any doubt that perfection does not and can not exist in this world of ours. Well, what is this then? - A masterpiece, what else could it be? The lyrics to it are beautiful too. Judge for yourself:

John Hendricks – I Remember Clifford Lyrics

I know he'll never be forgotten
He was a king uncrowned
I know I'll always remember

The warmth of his sound
Linger so long I'm sure he's still around
For those who heard they respect him yet
So those who hear won't forget

The sound of each phrase
Echoes the time uncountable by days
The things he played are with us now
And they'll endure should time allow

Oh yes I remember Clifford
I seem to always feel him near somehow
Every day I hear his lovely tone
In every trumpet sound that has a beauty all it's own

So how can we say someone so real has really gone away?
I hear him now, and always will
Believe me I remember Clifford still.

I REMEMBER CLIFFORD, ALONG CAME BETTY ....

I met Benny Golson in 1978 in Berlin. We arrived in the German capitol to take part in the historical reunion of several generations of the Messengers, which was to be televised all over Europe. Curtis Fuller, Reggie Workman, Bill Hardman, Benny Golson, Cedar Walton represented earlier editions of the Messengers. As I walked with my bags in the hotel lobby I saw a few people crowding around the check-in counter. "That's Benny Golson" said Art Blakey. He pointed at a gentleman standing in the crowd by the counter. Oh, my God, that's Benny Golson! He was one of the very few Jazz Heroes of mine whose audio and visual images had not merged for me yet. By then I had been playing I Remember Clifford at almost every concert for a year or so. And, of course, I had already been playing it in Moscow, way before leaving the USSR. I love the tune! It's a masterpiece! I love his other tunes too, don't get me wrong. Like, Along Came Betty, Are You Real?, all of his tunes actually. But that one is very special. It's dedicated to the memory of my greatest trumpet hero, Clifford Brown.

No big surprise, after a second tune of our set Art came up to the microphone and went into his usual "...we had been blessed with the best trumpet-players ..." etc. speech heralding my feature.

"Benny Golson is in the audience" flashed through my mind as the first chord of the intro was already ringing in the air. Television camera operators, a two thousand seat hall filled to capacity and millions of spectators in front of television sets around Western Europe held their breath - D, F, A, C, in eighth notes and the rest of the intro came out very clearly followed by 1, 2, 3, counted in my mind, then the melody came in on the fourth beat and sailed and sailed. What a beautiful tune! So Clifford Brown-like. It's a story, really. Keeps unfolding and unfolding, turning into an improvised solo........... *The sound of each phrase.... .... Every day I hear his lovely tone*

In every trumpet sound that has a beauty all it's own...................... Art Blakey's words about what a beautiful person Clifford Brown was - never any kind of arguments with anybody, soft-spoken, no drugs either are ringing in my mind. Trumpet solo ends - Bass solo, the trumpet comes in on the Bridge, Coda, Cadenza, Last note, Storm of applause. I open my eyes and see the gentleman I met in the morning of that day at the hotel. It's Benny Golson on the stage in front of me and applauding. "Thank you so much, Val. You played beautifully! Would you have time to join us after the concert?"

After the concert I went to the lounge downstairs. Benny Golson and a beautiful lady were already there and smiling at me. Mr. Golson was in his "work" outfit - the very stylish suit and tie he had on during the concert. But the lady was in a beautiful dress and wearing a lot of jewelry. Pearl necklaces, a wrist chain and bands, ruby, diamond and sapphire rings were gleaming and sparkling in their gold and platinum settings, emitting an exuberant aura of Jazz Royalty, Beauty, Taste and Success. Perfect illustration of Art Blakey's saying -

"IF YOU WANT TO KNOW HOW THE MAN IS DOING, LOOK AT HIS WIFE."

According to that philosophy Mr. Benny Golson was doing very well. I almost opened my mouth to say "Very nice meeting you Mrs. Betty Golson". Thank God Mr. Golson beat me to it with "Join us Val. Meet my wife Bobbie".

Bobbie? Not Betty! What sprang up in my mind was. "Uh - Oh, that was close!" They looked such a perfect couple, it was impossible to imagine B.G. dedicating his beautiful tune to someone else. Not his wife. Judging from how many people around the world love Benny Golson's music I had no doubt that the situation I just described had repeated itself time and again. Who is Betty then? I gotta find out.

This is what the answer turned out to be:

"Her name was Betty Prichet from Dayton, Ohio. I fell in love with her when I met her, and thought we would marry. It was then that I wrote the song. But one day I woke up and she was gone. My dream was shattered. But later I met a girl named Bobbie in Washington, DC. Not waiting too long, I married her and that was over 60 years ago. When we first married she was always with me, and when fans approached us, they shook my hand, then turned to her and said, "And you must be BETTY" Oh-h-h NO-O-O!!!"

Benny Golson.

I was lucky that Benny Golson saved me a lot of embarrassment and turned our conversation in another direction.

"You played 'I Remember Clifford' beautifully".

"Thank you Mr. Golson. I was playing it already in Moscow."

"Are there Performing Rights Organizations in Moscow, which collect royalties, like BMI or ASCAP in the US?"

Mr. & Mrs. Golson

Mrs. Bobbie Golson

"MUSIC COMES FROM GOD THROUGH MUSICIANS ON THE BAND STAND TO YOU THE AUDIENCE."

I still see and hear in my mind Art Blakey saying it to the jazz fans. Yes, music is a blessing. Where is this blessing coming from? - God, where else? Everything comes from God: light, air, water, day and night, stars, time, sound, music............

"IF YOU KNOW THE TRUTH, DON'T BE AFRAID TO SAY IT."

This is a very deep statement Art used to repeat and repeat. I think he was fascinated with it.

Truth is Sacred, Immense, Unconditional, Pure, Sublime, Majestic. Trying to alter the Truth, to misrepresent it, deface it, step upon it is stupid, criminal, playing with the danger of being eventually denounced, disgraced, disrespected and defeated. There is no secret in the world that remains a secret forever. Isn't that the Truth?

In Music precision is the Truth. Wrong notes, wrong chords, wrong roots, unsteady time, wrong emotion, etc. is a lie. The best musicians always play with the highest degree of precision. Charlie Parker, John Coltrane, Clifford Brown, Oscar Peterson, Herbie Hancock, Sonny Rollins, Wayne Shorter etc.

Blakey always played with the highest degree of precision. I never heard him giving way to circumstances. - Lack of sleep, fatigue, long travel, personal problems, whatever other considerations would've distracted somebody else, had never had any effect on him. They never altered his impeccable time and sense of music as a collective product creating the best environment for the Messengers to display their talents and potential. All editions of the Jazz

Messengers played their hearts out, individually and collectively, with the highest degree of precision and played their absolute best when they were with Art. As beautifully as they may have played with other bands or their own ones, no one played on the same level as when they were with Art Blakey.

"I BELIEVE IN THIS MUSIC BECAUSE IT'S THE TRUTH. ANYTHING THAT THE TRUTH FALLS ONTO, IT'LL GRIND IT TO POWDER. BUT IT TAKES A LONG TIME. YOU DON'T CHANGE HORSES IN MIDSTREAM. I TRY TO TEACH (THAT TO) ALL MY MUSICIANS."

ART BLAKEY

Truth is best. Truth is the easiest thing to say. Truth is stranger than fiction. If you know the truth don't be afraid to say it.

Truth is the best description of the music of the Messengers I can think of. No fake emotion, no pretension, no showing off, no "milking" the audience, no affectation, etc . Only real emotion.

The music of the Messengers - Hard Fought Victory, Beauty, Wisdom, Honor, Truth, ...Just take a look at the titles of the tunes the Messengers played: Tell It Like It Is, Moanin', I Remember Clifford, Are You Real? Crisis, Ping-Pong, Freedom Rider, Free For All, The CORE (Congress of Racial Equality), Justice (Evidence), Blues March, ...Mayreh, Backstage Sally, Along Came Betty, "Sincerely, Diana" etc. That's why Art, just like Ray Charles, loved songs with beautiful lyrics. There are no mere titles in the Messengers' repertoire either - there is always something behind the name of a tune, taken from real life experience.

Moanin', I Remember Clifford, Are You Real? Tell It Like It Is, Justice (Evidence) - These titles are self-explanatory and don't need to be spelled out. I had been fascinated with the album Moanin' ever since I heard it for the first time in Russia and particularly with the title tune. I conceder this album the best album ever recorded. All the tunes, arrangements, solos, precision, dynamics, intensity, emotional charge, you name it, everything is from a land of Divine, Unearthly, Beauty, I hear Wisdom, Good Will, Power, Moaning, Tragedy, Message, Direction, Hard Fought Victory, Blessing, Prayer, Confidence...........

Yes, Art did say more than once "Music Comes From God through the musicians on the band stand to you the audience". I really think it comes through him (Art) first, then to musicians on the band stand etc. Of course I asked AB about Moanin' the Album and Moanin', the album and song, about how they were created and recorded.

"We recorded everything, but still were short of one tune. So, Bobby (Timmons) went to the toilet and came out with Moanin." A joke obviously. Such a tune just like that? I laughed my heart out. And then Art came up with details:

"It came out of a call Bobby used to play at the end of a break between sets. He would go on the band stand and play it. Just a couple of notes out of the gospel music he used to play as a very young man in church, where his grandfather was a minister. So, the messengers would know the break was over and it's time to start a new set. So, out of those three notes Bobby built an A section, Benny (Golson) helped to write the Bridge and the song was ready." Surprise, Surprise! Who would've thought, that was the story!

When I was in the band Art Blakey used to go on a band stand and just click the tip of his cymbal, "Tsing". By the time I could make my way through the thick crowd of jazz fans filling every nook and cranny of a club, almost everybody who was supposed to be on the band stand was already there, picking up their instruments and getting ready.

Nowadays I lead a big band ("Our Father Who Art Blakey" AKA VPJBB or Valery Ponomarev Jazz Big Band). When it's time to go back on the bandstand, I come up to the piano and play Moanin'. It is no longer just a call consisting of a couple of notes but one of the most spiritual songs ever written and known all over the world. No need to look for each and every member of the band and tell them "Break is over, time to play", etc. Ah, ha. If I had to collect every band member of our 16 piece Big Band at the end of a break to tell them we start in 5 minutes, I would have to go to several places: the bar next door, the convenience store down the street, the pizzeria further down, any and all of the jazz clubs near by etc. By the time I finish all the rounds not only would the break be over, but most of the time for the set would be gone. No way, I would never do that. I am a Messenger, I got my schooling. By the time I finish the first A section half the band is already there. Sometimes even before I finish making myself comfortable on the piano bench and play the first sounds I see my buddies making their way through a thick crowd of the club's patrons. Some just appear on the band stand as if out of thin air. It always works. Try it sometimes.

As many times as I have spelled out to a new sub the meaning of my sitting behind the piano and playing Moanin' at the end of a break before the next set and where this custom came from, there is always somebody who didn't know it yet. Brother! Don't I have grand time telling and retelling the story of Moanin'? Love it!

Crisis by Freddie Hubbard is another story. As many times as I ask the audience, or even musicians, they have no idea what the song is all about. If I give a clue and say we are talking about 1962 and Cuba etc. somebody may guess what I am talking about. But far from always. It's about the Cuban missile crisis of 1962.

At the time I was too young to understand how close it really was. But I do remember that (there was a persistent rumor) Moscow citizens were just about to start receiving insert pages for their passports with instructions on where and how to evacuate, which train stations to go to and what trains to take etc. Did Freddie Hubbard know all these details? I don't think so. But he knew the "Crisis" was real. He knew that Humanity had arrived at a cliff and was ready to throw itself into the abyss. It's all in the tune. It really is. Think about it before you play it or listen to it the next time. I definitely hear tension building and building, rising and rising, looming danger getting closer and closer and then exploding.

"**Freedom Rider**" - It's about black people fighting for their rights to ride on interstate buses without being obligated to use the back row only, but being free to choose any seat on the bus - front, window, by the door etc. anywhere. Free for all. It's all in that incredible solo by Art Blakey.

"**Free For All**" is another tune from the Messengers' repertoire. Wayne Shorter wrote it.

"**The CORE**" (Congress of Racial Equality) by Freddie Hubbard. - It expresses the composer's admiration of that organization for its work for total, meaningful equality. Getting at the core, at the center of the kinds of change that have to take place before American society is really open to everyone. The piece was called that way as well because the music of the Messengers springs up from, is founded on the core of jazz, its feelings and its rhythms.

"**Blues March**" - did you know that this is a beautiful picture of a brass band walking through the streets "painted" for us with his musical brushes by Benny Golson?

If you ever heard a brass band marching through streets, you remember that what you heard first was sounds of drums approaching from distance. You couldn't even see the band yet. Then trumpets. You turn in the direction of those enchanting sounds and, lo and behold, there are ranks in files of musicians with instruments marching in your direction, drawing nearer and nearer. And then it's not just trumpets or trombones, tubas nor saxophones, flutes, clarinets - it's one mass of sound enveloping everything. Then the band walks away and the most natural diminuendo is taking charge until the roaring of just moments ago turns into a hardly discernible melody and then even that fades away. But you still hear drums. Yes, you hear drums the last and then the sounds of the streets take over. Remember Art Blakey's intro to Blues March and how the tune ends?

A lot of people think that "**Ping-Pong**" by Wayne Shorter is another tune reflecting the political atmosphere of the time. But no, it can't be. The first breakthrough in China-USA relationships happened in 1971 and ended a long isolationist stand. That's when Chinese authorities allowed the American table tennis team to enter their country. But Wayne Shorter wrote his beautiful tune in 1961. So, the tune has to be about the game then. I do see two players with paddles passing the ball back and forth across the table when I hear the Messengers playing Ping-Pong. (No pun intended). I will ask Mr. Shorter about his tune when and if I have a chance. I love the tune anyway.

Once upon a time Horace Silver saw a beautiful girl. What's your name, he asked, **"Mayreh"** she said.

You mean to say Mary, right? Horace made sure he understood the girl correctly.

Yes, she said, Mayreh.

As it turned out, her name was Mary. It's just the way she pronounced it. So, Horace Silver named his new tune just like that and it went down in Jazz History after Art Blakey, Curly Russell, Horace Silver, Lou Donaldson and Clifford Brown played and recorded it for Blue Note records at the legendary jazz club Bird Land. The recording came out as "A Night At Birdland" and helped to lay down the way for the new jazz style - the genre called Hard Bop. Not to mention that the recording became one of the most loved Jazz Albums of all time. It is History now. So is the girl named *Mayreh*.

Some seven years later it was a different girl, but the story of ***Backstage Sally*** is very similar. There was a young lady hanging out backstage every time the Messengers played at Birdland. This time it was Wayne Shorter who asked her name. Sally was the answer. You guessed the rest. That's where Wayne Shorter got the idea for the title of his new tune - Backstage Sally. It was also performed and recorded for Blue Note Records at Birdland and came out on

Buhaina's Delight (1961). Needless to say it's one of the most loved albums among jazz fans and a legend. So is Sally.

"Along Came Betty" - judging from the melody, whoever miss Betty was, she must've had a beautiful walk. Just like the Brazilian girl I met at JFK before flying to Rio de Janeiro in March 1977. No, no, just like the one walking along the bank of Sienna River in Paris. Noooooooo.................it's the one I saw in Tokyo walking right at me. Brazilian and Parisian girls were kinda similar looking - not tall, muscular, feminine muscular, slim, wiry, agile, elegant, with dance like movements, very pretty. But the Japanese one was very untypical of her stock - tall and full bodied, wide boned, as a Muscovite would've said. Big, but perfect proportions. The young lady walked radiating confidence. She was about nineteen, maybe twenty at the most, but already used to people gawking at her. What if she was a model? They are certainly used to people staring at them. Models don't always have to be tall and slim. Somebody has to demonstrate dresses for big women too. Any way, that regal walk of hers was something else. What kind of a walk did Betty have?

I had heard Art delivering the statement **"Truth is stranger than fiction"** during concerts many times. Sometimes coupled with

"MUSIC WASHES AWAY THE DUST OF EVERYDAY LIFE."

I am absolutely sure that it had been repeated time after time for us, the musicians on the band stand, more than for the audience. Yes, music puts us in touch with deeper or even the deepest grottoes of our being. It cuts through all of the layers our daily routine envelopes us into, past our numbed senses, right to the core.

You think that's far fetched? Not at all. How about when a solution to a problem you were trying to work out all day long jumps out at you in a dream. Yes, when you sleep. That's because all the other distractions of the previous day are absent. Street noise, other concerns, responsibilities, errands, duties, people around you, whatever those distractions might've been are no longer there. Your body rests, you are relaxed, but the brain is still at work and it's one on one with a problem you were trying to solve. That's why you see dreams to begin with.

It happens at one time or another to everyone. A painter "sees" his painting, astronomer "discovers" new star, an archeologist "digs out" buried treasure, a composer "hears" a new melody, etc. etc. These "enigmatic" "premonitions", these "mysterious" prognostications are commonplace. The same with music. For musicians and the audience. We had already talked about it a few pages ago. Incidentally, that's how Art Blakey played. When he was playing nothing else mattered, nothing would distract him. Music was reigning supreme, that's all that mattered. Everything else was left outside of the stage.

"MUSIC IS LIKE A RIVER; IT'S SUPPOSED TO FLOW AND WASH AWAY THE DUST OF EVERYDAY LIFE. MUSIC GOES TO THE CYCLE. BUT IT'S GOT TO COME BACK TO THE TRUTH."

- ART BLAKEY.

Ever since I sat in with the Messengers for the first time the feeling of being a part of something very special has always stayed with me. In his own way Art would remind us that Music is much more then just melodies, scales, theory etc. Don't mess around or...................I heard AB providing an answer to that riddle too. Here it is -

"God gave you talent - use it (practice, learn, listen, perform etc.). *If you don't, he will take it away from you!"*

The way he was delivering this sermon, it sounded like the worst punishment there could ever be. You know right away, you don't want to suffer from that one. To endure something of that magnitude. Oh, no, please......................

In a manner of encouragement or a reinforcement of that idea or, maybe, instruction on how to go about it and avoid the "punishment" Art would often say:

"ONCE YOU ARE A MESSENGER, YOU ARE ALWAYS A MESSENGER."

Like a member of Parliament, Doctor, Professor, Ambassador. Not an ex Messenger.

"IF YOU WERE GREAT ONCE, YOU GOTTA KEEP ON PROVING IT."

In other words if you were born an eagle, you should remain an eagle.

"IF YOU DON'T APPEAR - YOU DISAPPEAR."

(Playing in public, hanging out, putting out CD's etc.)

"TO DIE IS EASY. TO LIVE IS A TRICK"

I heard this many times, just like most of Art's educational statements. Usually he was talking about one old timer or other who used to play his heart out some years previously but now...

Don't rest on your laurels. That's what he meant.

At one time Art said this about Miles Davis. The way I saw it at first was that Art couldn't agree with anyone becoming inactive, just not wanting to play. Not Art. He was always ready to play, to drive to a concert location or fly anywhere in the world. So, when the rumor had it, that Miles stopped playing, did not go out anywhere, just lounged around in his house and partied with ladies, Art was, of course, bewildered. "Why wouldn't he just put the mute in his trumpet and book himself a gig at Vanguard. People would mob the club." Later I realized that he was actually throwing out ideas for us to consider. The way I see it now is that one can not just keep on reliving the past.

Yes, you are a Messenger as of 20 or 30 years ago. But what are you doing now? Who is going to come out and pay money to hear you play if you are no longer as good as you used to be, if you haven't practiced your craft for years? With so many young musicians coming on the scene, you will be a "has been". According to the popular cliché " a truckload of tenor-players arrive in New York City every day". One could've easily added "great tenor-players, talented, outstanding talents, full of ideas, eager to prove themselves, eager to learn". Go ahead, compete with them. Meaning that you keep on performing in public. But if you are not, for whatever reason it might be, your name fades away. Literally disappears. Just like Art used to say "If you don't appear, you disappear".

I am trying to think of what makes musicians not play any more. But instead Benny Golson's name keeps coming up in my mind. At the time of this writing he is 90 and a half years old and playing his heart out all over the world: Singapore, Spain, Germany, Russia, boat cruises you name it. Doc Cheatham held a steady gig at Sweet Basil at the age of 90 every Sunday. I heard him there, live. He sounded beautiful. I wish I had taken a lesson from him. He knew how to play trumpet, he really knew all the secrets. Clark Terry, the same.

John Coltrane was continuously digging deeper and deeper into the vastness of "Musical Infinity". Sonny Rollins got himself off the scene for a couple of years to work out new ideas. As the saying goes, he was "shedding." So did Miles Davis. He came back with a vengeance. I loved his new music. Not exactly Jazz, as everybody thought it should sound. It was new music for a new generation. Young people mobbed his concerts in the States and around the world, not even knowing that he was a Jazz superstar. Yes, the music was new and referred to as "Rock"? But in the band were always some of the most prominent jazz soloists of the day: sax players Bill Evans, Kenny Garrett, Bob Berg ...Wasn't it when the tradition of the best jazz artists of the day joining famous rock groups started. Should we accredit this innovation to Miles? Ha! What an idea! After all it was Miles who throughout his career kept on moving from one latest style to another, one and then to another, then to another. Be Bop, Cool, Hard Bop, Avant-garde, Free, etcetera, etcetera...and ending up with the latest variation of "Rock", whatever the critics label it, style. No matter how you look at it, but Miles certainly did not disappear. He did not rest on his already huge (at every juncture) laurels.

"MUSIC IS A COLLECTIVE PRODUCT"

Hearing it at first I thought it was obvious. We were a sextet, so, naturally, it took six of us to play our program. And then step by step the wisdom of this statement reveled itself to me. It's a collective product on many levels. Look at it this way - if I mess up my part, or any of the horn players do, it doesn't mean that just that particular part is unusable. The whole arrangement is a mess. Regardless of how perfectly everybody else played their parts. Collective product! Somebody played just a fraction of the initial statement out of tune - the whole number is wasted. Very often the whole concert goes down the drain, musically speaking.

It starts from the beginning. From the very first tune, from the band coming in. Everybody knows the cue. Everybody is ready to come in. Just one person coming in late, which is worse than not coming in at all, and the quality of the opener and of the whole concert has already gone all the way down. For everybody, not just for the one who forgot why he is on the stage and holding his instrument.

You want to know what Art Blakey used to say on this subject? Here -

"WHEN IT'S TIME TO COME IN, YOU COME IN."

Art - "One time Lee Morgan was in the toilet (the toilet again) when I was playing the cue for the head out. He jumped out of the WC playing and came in perfectly in time, anyway".

Very often musicians do not understand how important the arrangement is and concentrate only on their own solo. Here we go, a collective product again. If the arrangement is not executed clearly, solos lose their potential and start to sound out of place, not related to anything.

Ultimately, what is improvisation? An artist is improvising on something. In the case of a jazz musician he improvises on a tune most of the time. A dancer may improvise on his ballet part, a dance form, on a cha-cha or tango. An actor in a play may, and very often does, improvise on his part. Improvisation is everywhere. Literature, sports, stand-up comedy, anything. Speech is an improvisation. A boxer or a hockey player never sticks exactly to the plan worked out for him and the team by his trainer. He always improvises on what had been prepared for a particular event and practiced during training sessions. (Very often excruciating ones.)

How is it then "Speech is an improvisation"? - Very simple. You speak on the same subject very often. You discuss the same political or sporting event, describe the same movie, a scene, landscape, personal issues etc. with different friends all the time. Right? Do you always use exactly the same wording. Of course not. It's always different, but the idea remains the same. You improvise on an idea without even thinking about it. Very often you are looking for another way to express the same thought when your audience don't seem to follow you in a conversation, presentation, lecture or sermon. You are improvising.

What did Art Blakey say on the subject?

Of course I have one for you. Just like all the other Blakey "postulates", I've heard this one many times. Here -

"THERE IS MORE THAN ONE WAY TO SKIN A CAT."

Yes, That's another one I have heard from Art so many times, that is still ringing in my ears. Its equivalent is "Variety is the spice of Life". No, I never heard him using this variation, but the meaning is almost the same.

"All eighth notes, the whole solo, just eighth notes" a new friend of mine, a budding jazz bassist, commented as he and I were listening to, not Paganini's Perpetual Mobile, but to a Jazz trumpet solo played by a very well known musician. (I don't want to identify him.) No breaks, except for an intake of breath, the same scale up and down, all the same, on and on and on. The same volume, the same articulation tra-ta-ta-ta-ta all the way. Wasn't that boring?! I have heard piano solos executed in the same manner - the same emotional charge, the same triple forte dynamic, the same scale on and on, just like a machine gun - tra-ta-ta-ta-ta , the whole gig like that. Drummers too, not accompanying a soloist, not going along with what's being played, but banging and banging through every solo in total violation of "Music is a collective product" too. No matter how many soloists there are in the band on every tune, different ones, the drummer is still playing the same very paradiddle totally unrelated to the lines, phrases and forms being performed. Haven't I heard that enough? What sense does that make? Boring audiences to "death"!

"It's modern jazz" some may say. Sorry, not "may" say, but they "do" say that very often: "You don't understand modern Jazz", it's Another Art Form, a New Kind.

Yeah, sure. All good words, but they don't apply. Music is still music, art, High Art. Whether it's Classical Music or Jazz, it's supposed to adhere to the same musical laws and express just as wide range of emotion. Speaking of a wide range of expression. How about Niccolo Paganini? His playing of tender passages was so beautiful that audiences often burst into tears, and yet, he could perform with such force, ferocity and dexterity that some listeners became half crazed.

The same for Jazz. Variety, many ways to "skin a cat". The range of human emotion alone is already an unbounded hemisphere. Dynamics, trills, tremolos, short phrases, long phrases, vertical ones, horizontal ones, the use of scales, (inside/outside ones), forms, chords, chord progressions, harmonic sequences, melodic ones, rhythmic sequences, both, rhythmic patterns .... and on, and on, and on. Digging into that treasure chest more and more, deeper and deeper - that's what gives a performer, composer a chance to engage the audience so it will become one with the musicians on stage, become a part of the "alloy", of music as a collective product.

Get this! Blakey was not talking about music only. The "There is more than one way ......" concept applies to anything. I don't need to convince you that cooking, for example, involves improvisation. Some cooks are incredible improvisers and create wonders out of limited available ingredients or demonstrate inconceivable inventiveness finding and using different components, sometimes unheard of plants, roots, seeds, weeds, you name it.

How about dress designers? I tell you. If not for these guys, we would still be walking around in animal skins. Forget about different fabrics, colors, patterns, shapes and forms, designs. Just put on your good old bear skin and go about your business. No fashion shows either. Everybody is dressed the same. Designing anything implies invention/improvisation.

How about car mechanics? In those situations when factory built spare parts are not available, some of them will stun you with their resourcefulness and build a replacement out of bits and pieces, trash really, you would've never thought could be useful for anything. And the list goes on and on and on............

Enough of eighth notes. There is more than one way to play a solo. It's not about music only. How about this one? - There is a solution. No matter how desperate or hopeless a situation may seem, there is a way out. You just didn't think of it yet. Every puzzle has a solution. It may not always be laying around on a surface, but it's there. Just try to see it from another angle. Sleep on it. "Morning is wiser than Evening." - A Russian saying.

If you are not convinced yet, try to "skin a cat" this way: At a moment when you are truly lost and don't know how to deal with a situation ask yourself "What do I do here?" or "What is the answer to this question?" and a solution will come. Unexpectedly. Out of nowhere, just like that. It might even take you a moment to realize that the answer had already come, but you missed it. The trick here is this - put up a question to yourself. Do not ask anybody else. Otherwise you will be dealing with a saying "Don't ask no question, you will be told no lies".

Back to "Music is a collective Product".

In Jazz, improvisation is an integral part of the idiom, taken for granted. Every musician is expected to take an improvised solo. There are some jazz big band musicians who do not play even slight variations on a theme, but stick to their parts only, devoting themselves exclusively to section playing. But that is an exception to the rule. Otherwise everybody in jazz improvises. Whether it's one musician who solos and the rest accompany, or everybody in the band improvises collectively. It is a Collective Product again. It might seem that one or more band members are not involved and are just staying around, waiting for their chance to play their story. No, no, don't be fooled. He or she is very much a part of it knowing exactly where in the form and chord progression the band is. Not just him. Everybody. Collective Product it is. You thought I was taking it a little too far. Not at all, I am not even done yet. What else could it be? You mean you don't know? How about the audience? Don't you forget that one.

The audience participates on equal terms with the musicians on the band stand.

"RESPECT THE AUDIENCE. DON'T TAKE THE AUDIENCE FOR A FOOL."

You know who I've heard it from a "zillion" times. A.B., of course.

The audience is involved in your performance even before you arrive at the venue. How? Very simple. A promoter very often lets you know or you hear it from your agent, a friend might call you for help to get a ticket. One way or the other you will hear these famous "Leads": "All the tickets are sold out." "Sales are very poor." "A lot of tickets sold right before the show."

That alone already sets the mood for the oncoming encounter with the Musical Spirits.

Audience participation is present in any form of art. But particularly in Jazz. Here! A concert is just about to begin. An announcement goes off "Dear ladies and gentlemen ....Art Blakey and the Jazz Messengers" The concert venue explodes. The crowd is roaring in anticipation and cheering you on before you have even found your spot on the band stand. Oh, yes, that will set the mood for the concert. Of course you are always playing your heart out whether there is a lot of people there or just one fan sitting somewhere in the corner. But the vibe coming from the space in front of you does make a big difference.

The band is "burning", the audience are clapping their hands in rhythm with the music on two and four, shaking their heads, stomping their feet, whistling and screaming, even verbally communicating with the artists. The scene is "happening". The charge is intensifying, "the voltage" is getting higher and higher. From the band stand to the people, from the people to the band stand and on and on. Like an alternating current from the stage to the audience and back again. Who is charging whom? It does not matter. The spirits are flying high, music is reigning supreme. The Collective Product is in full bloom.

Whether one learned and practiced the "tricks" of the trade very well or had never really investigated what it is behind those beautiful solos played by the masters, everybody blows his/her heart out. Improvises. On what?

The concept of improvisation implies that you embellish, turn around, adorn, present in a new or different light something given. Melody, that's what we are almost always dealing with. What a great source or basis for creating one's own input in the performance. Why? Because melody includes in itself everything required for composing music. There are form, phrase, harmony, roots, rhythm. A lot of melodies have lyrics to them. Here is an idea for composing/improvising your solo too. Emotion. How about that? Music without emotion? No way. Not only music. No form of art without projecting and invoking emotion could be considered art.

Every band member improvises on the same tune, right? Here is your collective product again. OK, how about just one musician, say a bass-player hits a wrong note. Which means that the chord at the given moment won't sound right. It's a negative impact on the performance for everybody. Not just the bass - player. You guessed it. Collective Product gain.

The same goes for any single instrument whether in a duo, trio...quintet or a 100 piece Philharmonic Orchestra. Let's say a trumpet player cracked a note playing in a section. The whole piece is messed up, not just this particular trumpet part. The same if it was a trumpet solo with the band accompanying. What happens very often is this: the piano-player hits a wrong chord while accompanying a soloist, say flute. So, the note written in the solo part does not fit the chord any more. The flute player's first reaction is to "tune in", in to a wrong chord that is and - Crack-Crack-Crack. Oh, boy, it sounds ugly! The listener thinks right away that the virtuoso, who has a lot of credits under his belt, according to the program any way, must be drunk, or the promoters lied, or the fellow with a flute did not learn his part or whatever. But the truth is - it's not even the flutist's fault.

Wait, wait, wait, I am not finished. Pitch, time, entrances are the same for everybody too. Alright! How about dynamics, articulation, registers? Volume? Oh, yes. I can write a book on that one. I have met musicians who never understood balance. Volume balance, that is. This guitar player or that bass player or a horn player would blare his brains out no matter what. It's just a twisted concept of sound. Good sound is quality sound, not loud sound. Is it because one always needs to stick out? Be heard above everybody or just hard of hearing? Regardless of music being projected. Guitar-players, obviously influenced by rock, are very often guilty of playing too loud.

Some pick up the idea of balance right away, some never do. Some piano-players and bass-players rely on amplifiers to the extent that the collective product suffers a lot. They worry about their fingers, forgetting about the other players and the ultimate - the CP. To play with someone like that is unbearable sometimes. It's a real trial. No matter how many times you indicate (without the audience being aware of it, naturally) that the volume is too high, it remains or comes back to right where it was.

The most guilty of it are the sound engineers. Of course. But again, they are not musicians. Most of them never studied music or even the sound engineering business and totally misunderstand what they are dealing with.

Try to explain to him that "Music is a Collective Product." He gets back at you with "You are playing trumpet. It's an acoustic instrument". Yes, sure, but so are all other instruments. Bass, Drums, Piano, all winds etc. all are acoustic instruments. If you bring up the volume of a single one, you have to amplify all of them just as much. Otherwise the natural balance is lost. Jazz is acoustic music and sprung up in a totally natural environment, at a time when there wasn't any kind of amplification, none. Nature provided the balance.

Here comes today's sound engineer and tries to mess with Nature. Oh, please! The first thing he does is to bring up the piano and bass volume, then drums, then vocal, etc. The last one he deals with is trumpet. If it was anywhere above zero on the sound board dial, he brings that one all the way down and gives you the classic "Don't worry Mr. Ponomarev, we hear you very well." As many times as I tried to explain that I need to hear myself on the stage, not in the hall, to be able to perform, he comes back with the same

"Don't worry......." business etc. No monitors help either. I wonder what Louis Armstrong would've said to that. I assume he could've commented on that because amps and microphones were already widely used towards the end of his life. I just never heard of it. I read of Rafael Mendez losing his temper over a band being too loud while he was playing. Between studio work, master classes, concerts, TV appearances etc, etc, he was a very busy musician. There was no way he could afford swollen chops.

I've never met a sound engineer who knew the difference between volume and projection. Trumpet sound, even at mezzo forte, projects further than any other instrument. It's just because the air stream formed in its horizontal tubing cuts through space and travels further. Saxophone sound, for example, comes out of the tone holes and the bell, which is very short and turned upward, not forward, any way. It's the nature of the instrument.

Now you try to explain to the sound "authority" that the trumpet is not supposed to be played loud. Otherwise one's chops do not function (or in trumpet player language don't buzz,) then they get sore, the sound gets distorted and then there is no sound anymore coming out of the trumpet at all and a trumpet player is upset and uptight. I've seen even great trumpet players getting mad and brawling with those responsible for the sound at the venue. There is a video on YouTube of Miles Davis pointing at his ear in attempt to show the sound engineer that he does not hear himself.

Miles Davis communicating w. sound engineer

Did you ever experience speaking in a noisy surroundings when the noise suddenly cuts off. What happens then? You realize that you were screaming on top of your lungs in a very coarse voice. Oh. Boy, it's embarrassing. You start apologizing in a husky voice and even cough. The same with a trumpet-player. When all the instruments around him are loud he subconsciously raises his volume. It's called over blowing. And then missed notes, husky sound, no sound, injured chops etc. All because of that Sound Pest, that Plague, the so-called Authority at work. Just as I described above.

Have I made enough enemies by now? Well. "If you know the Truth, don't be afraid to say it". Right?

OK.

Have I already mentioned enough times that speaking and playing a wind instrument, or learning your first language and learning to play are almost identical processes? Playing and singing too.

"DYNAMICS GUYS, DYNAMICS"

Out of all Art Blakey's postulates, this one was used the most.

Dynamics! Oh, yes. Didn't you notice that listening to some great players you catch yourself getting bored. What's wrong? You might think. There are recordings, even by greatest of players, which I can not listen to for longer than a couple of minutes. What's wrong? I will tell you what's wrong.

Dynamics. Dynamics guys, dynamics. The recordings I am talking about are overcharged with the same level of emotion. Sometimes highest possible excitement, sometimes "searching" and "philosophical", but all the way through from opening statement to solos to coda, all the same. The mind gets bored and tired.

Variety is the spice of life. That's what keeps the listener on alert and attracts the audience's attention. PPP and FFF are there for a reason. Not just them. The high register, intensity, lower register, fast runs and sostenuto. Long solos, short solos. A diversity of chords and substitutions from "inside" through the furthest "outside", keys. Slow tempos, fast tempos, different rhythms all are there for a reason, to create colorful, not a monotone picture.

"Just like Music Is A Collective Product" has very many levels to it. So is Diversity.

"DON'T PUT ALL YOUR EGGS IN ONE BASKET."

- ART BLAKEY

I heard that one in Brazil on my first tour with the Messengers. Excited?

Who wouldn't be excited? With the Messengers! In Brazil! Staying in one of the high-rises which are stretched out along the Atlantic Ocean shore like tin soldiers all the way to the horizon on the right and on the left. The famous Copacabana beach was right in front of the windows of my hotel room. A little distance further to the right I could see even more famous Ipanema beach. Yes, that beach where the Girl From Ipanema came from.

I always thought that the heroine of the world's most famous song was a fictional character or at least existed in some other dimension of glory and beauty, not in the everyday life of ours. What a surprise it was to find out, when I was already back to New York City, that the Girl From Ipanema was a real person and still hung out on that very beach. She was no longer young but a bloated elderly lady and still hanging on to her past glory pushing the sand with her swollen feet and introducing herself to the beach goers. She had a name too. Nicknamed Helô when she was an eighteen year-old young lady from the neighborhood named Heloisa Eneida Menezes Pais Pinto. Her walk was sheer poetry.

There were so many girls passing by on the way to and from the beach. Any one of them could pass for Jobim's "heroine". He used to watch that poetry of a walk sitting at a café near by.

Any way, with all of that plus playing every night with Art Blakey behind you how could you not blow your brains out? What's wrong with you? I sure did and totally lost track of the beautifully constructed Clifford Brown's solos of which I transcribed so many. Here comes "professor in residence" Art Blakey himself:

"Wayne (Shorter) used to be like that" And then Art followed with a whole presentation. "You see, you don't need to play 20 choruses to make your point. I was there when Charlie Parker played just an 8 bar solo, just 8 bars, and the audience exploded".

I know what you, my dear reader, are going to say. How about Coltrane blowing set-long solos?

Yes, John Coltrane did solo some times on one tune for the duration of a whole set. That's true. He must've been in some kind of a sound zone, enveloped in the excitement of exploring further and further, deeper and deeper into the endless vastness of musical space. After all, Coltrane had an astoundingly diverse vocabulary. Taken into account, this allowed him to keep on playing and break the rules. Every rule gets broken anyway. That's why there are exceptions to rules.

Miles Davis, after one of Coltrane's particularly long explorations, asked him why are you playing such long solos.

"I just can't stop" was the answer.

"Did you ever try taking the mouthpiece out of your mouth?" Miles Davis wondered.

So, what is the point of this lecture?

Every musician needs to learn the laws of constructing a solo, or, better still, telling a story. I did not misuse the term, but deliberately brought up the literary parallel. I have already brought up the parallel in this book. Remember? The process of learning to play an instrument is identical, not similar, to learning to speak a language. "U", U", "M", M" followed by Uuu, Uuu, "Ma, Ma" etc. Remember? A beautiful solo played on a musical instrument is like a beautiful story written by a very good writer. Both are constructed according to the same rules. In other words, learn the rules of constructing solos, then free yourself from them, break them. It can't be done in reverse. One cannot be free of something if he does not know what it is. An example? Sure - how can you be free of harmony if you don't know it? The same goes for form, phrase, pitch, time, dynamics, articulation etc. Coltrane sure knew them all very well. So, he had all of it and could break any and all of them. It doesn't work the other way around.

I will definitely expand this topic in my next book, but right now I will give you a few pointers. Or look at it like a home work assignment and then compare your research with my presentation. I bet you will discover many a pattern in composing music or writing a story on your own. I hope you, my dear reader, will find these next couple of paragraphs interesting, whether you are a musician or not. Any way, the pointers :

Check out any solo which made the strongest impact on you, the one that generated the strongest emotions. Why emotions? We have already talked about this one too. "How do you tell the difference between art and pretentious junk ?" Remember? Take almost any Charlie Parker solo,

Clifford Brown's, pre avant-garde John Coltrane, Oscar Peterson, Wynton Kelly, Bill Evans, Miles Davis, Wayne Shorter, Lee Morgan, Jackie McLean, etc. See how the solo is constructed - initial statement, development, build up, tension - resolution, from one to several peaks, each succeeding one more intense, "higher", than the previous one, resolution, final statement.

What are the means of building tension? - faster runs, higher register, dynamics. Check out the use of melodic material, one bar, two bar, four bar phrases - speech particles, words, sentences, call and response, rhythmic and melodic repetitions, quoting the melody being improvised on or another one on the same changes, or playing quotes from somebody else's solo. Why? I did mention it before. - Because the melody itself includes everything a musician needs for building his solo. All the building blocks are there: form, phrasing, dynamics, chords, time, rhythmic patterns etc.

Write a diagram, just like a line on a screen reflecting the ascending and descending of a production. But for our purposes the line going up signifies building up tension, dropping down > resolves, rising, building up tension again and going further > then dropping down > resolving. It's usually out of four three to one ratio.

Do some research, study how your favorite musical heroes worked on their solos well before they recorded them. You doubt Dizzy Gillespie, Clifford Brown, Freddie Hubbard, Lee Morgan (and the list goes on and on) worked on their solos prior to recordings? You do? Listen to alternate takes, then. Sometimes takes number 2, 3, 4 etc. are the exact repetitions of the main take or at least very similar in content, no matter how many takes there are available. What does it tell you? Your favorite, a musical hero of yours, worked very hard on this or that phrase, chord substitution, melodic or rhythmical pattern etc. in preparation for this particular recording session. In advance!

Have you ever heard some "teacher" saying, "think when you play?" OK, then. Try to think when the chords are already moving and passing by at the speed of at least 66 beats per minute. Go ahead, try to think what to play over that chord. It did take you a sec to figure out the chord. A sec at best. It may take much longer. OK, you came up with a decision. Now what are you going to play over it? Oh, yes? That phrase, those notes, that dynamic, that register, out of the "inside" scale, "outside"...??? How long will it take you to realize that the chord in question is already gone, you missed it already, a while ago! At best, if you worked on similar chord progression, form, etc. you might be able to work it out like a "puzzle", fast. But! It'll still take you a moment and the notes will sound not exactly in sync with the rest of the band. Particularly not with the rhythm section - the time, chords, pitch etc. Precision is definitely not there. The "Music Is a Collective Product Rule" is not even broken, but totally neglected and disrespected. Breaking rules is one thing. Neglecting them, disrespecting them is another.

"Think while you play"? - Nope, wrong! It is too late to think when you are already in the whirlpool of playing. But this doesn't cancel the thinking process at all. How? I just demonstrated it to you - you think before you play. For the most part well before you are in a playing/recording situation. Take it from the masters. You study everything, study well and you will never be caught again playing the same meaningless scales, all in eighth notes, or the same scale patterns chorus after chorus, again and again. And deceiving yourself or imagining yourself this great player or that one and boring the audience to death. **"Don't take an audience for a fool."** (**Art Blakey**) Alright ?

Thank you!

Diversity, variety is an incredible factor. One can experience its effects almost everywhere, not only music. Sports, Theater, Ballet, Painting etc. Food too. Don't eat the same foods every day.

"THE FIRST TAKE IS THE BEST ONE."

My first record with Art Blakey and the Jazz Messengers was "Gypsy Folk Tales". After recording the very first take Bobby (Watson), David (Schnitter), Dennis (Irwin) and I rushed to the recording engineer's room, impatient as we were, to hear what came out. Art walked in when the most sophisticated audio registering equipment I had ever seen up till that point was playing the very first recording of Gypsy Falk Tales' by Walter Davis and rolling it to the end of coda. "We can do better on the solos," somebody said.

"**Not guilty**" was Art Blakey's verdict. "Let's get on with the next tune. If the arrangement came out good, there is no need to do another take. You think you will play a better solo on the second or the third take. You think you made mistakes and want to correct them, you probably will, but then you will make new mistakes and find something else in the new solo you are unhappy about. Do you know what Miles (Davis) said at a recording session, when the sound engineer asked him to replay a tune, because the tapes were not running? 'We've played it already.' That's what he said. And that was it. They didn't come back to that tune even at the end of the session. The first take is always the best one." Bobby started saying something apologetically and heard "Just play your ass off, Bobby" for encouragement in response.

Yes, It has proven time and again that the display of emotion for the first time is always the freshest, the strongest, the truest, the most natural..........Not only in music. How about an interview? Somebody is asking you the same question again and again. The same joke is delivered to the same group of friends or audience. Try it. Somebody will always say, we've heard it already. Tell us something new. I always keep that in mind when an interviewer wants to rehearse before recording and expects an answer to the questions he had prepared. I always ask to wait until the tape rolls on. The answer always comes out best the first time.

"CONTROL YOUR EMOTIONS."

Oh, Boy, here we go! There is a lot to be said about this one. If you are in the arts - you will be dealing with emotions. On different levels and manifestations, but you will be dealing with them. It's just so.

It starts here - There is no any form of art, which does not express emotion or, I'd rather say, should. Otherwise it's not art but a depiction, exercise, report, document, description. Not art. When you experience art you gasp with awe. Art evokes goose bumps, fear, excitement, love, hatred, trust, confidence, belief .... Oscar Peterson's first teacher, his older sister Daisy Peterson Sweeney, recognized a future musical giant, an extraordinary artist in the young man from the emotion he was putting into the pieces he was practicing.

On the other hand if a painting, poem, play, dance, etc. leaves you absolutely indifferent, you can name it whatever you want, just do not call it a piece of art. Dealing with art makes an artist much more sensitive to the life around him. Out of the audio, visual, tactile/sensory/ intellectual, intuitive and emotional senses, that last one (emotion) becomes the dominant one for most artists. I'd say for musicians the audible, the sound is what triggers feelings the most deeply

There are some people who have all types of perception highly developed. Some have only one or two. I know people who react to life around them on emotional level only. What a funny bunch! No matter what goes on - buying potatoes at a farmers market, having a haircut, paying a telephone bill, playing sports, you name it, he or she is all worked up and agitated and puts his/her whole soul into it. On the other hand there are people who do not have any senses at all. None! I've met one. Not that he learned to keep his feelings to himself and not to show them to anybody. No, he just did not have any, period. This gentleman fancied himself a Jazz Critic. Can you imagine a music critic not having at least a decent ear (being able to hear)?

Not this guy. To paraphrase a Russian saying, this "critic" didn't know the difference between F# and a brick. He didn't know the difference between the tune Fair Weather and the name of the band Weather Report, he couldn't feel anything; no beautiful scenery, melody, poetry, lyrics, or painting would ever move him. The only thing you could hear from him was a repetition of somebody else' opinion. Which was always delivered with deep conviction and always out of context. It is a very rare extreme. You don't deal with something like that very often at all. But I was "lucky" and met a live person who absolutely did not need to read this chapter, nor hear Art Blakey's famous "Control your emotions".

But I do rather often see musicians going through all sorts of facial contortions trying to enact an emotion they think the performed piece should awake. I have heard and seen a piano player punching a C major triad out of his keyboard and acting up as if he was dealing with some kind of Mount Everest emotional peak. A cheap show for the sake of the audience, of course. As Art would've said **"Milking the audience"**. Very seldom does the audience fall for it, though. Another AB's saying comes handy here is **"Don't take the audience for a fool."**

Actors and musicians deal with emotions the most. Art Blakey took it as his responsibility to warn us about this impending problem or call it a noxious byproduct, which necessarily comes with being an artist and needs to be dealt with. **"Control your emotions. Learn to control your emotions"**. (A.B.) We all heard it coming from Art a lot. Not being able to is trouble. Art Blakey told me a story of Lee Morgan helplessly crying upon listening to a beautiful performance of a ballad. He did say what the recording in question it was, but my mind did not register it. I was so surprised at hearing it, because Lee Morgan, judging from his playing, was in my mind very strong and tough, projecting very strong emotion, of course. But crying! I have heard from people who knew him he was also a very good basketball player (sports and music again), wiry, outspoken, cocky..... WAW! Overwhelmed by what he was listening to and cried.......

Exponents of any artistic expression deal with excitement, exaltation, innervations, you name it. Actors actually learn in drama school to enact all sorts of human feelings. Not only learn, but practice during rehearsals and act out during performances, striving for the most realistic representation. Under this kind of an impact anybody's personality would be severely impacted. The same for musicians.

People experience nervous breakdowns, for different reasons, which have nothing to do with art. But artists, bombarded by all human experiences plus the demands of their profession, don't even notice how they can become high strung, short fuse, nervous wrecks, moody, thin-skinned....

No wonder they need to learn to deal with the sneaky the most, to harness these arts' unavoidable companions. The earlier, the better.

I have seen many an artist going off, losing it. My favorite ones too. I came face to face with this at my very first professional gig at the Moscow Drama Theatre, where I played trumpet in the pit. Not that I was at a crazy house, no. But every once in a while I watched from the pit incredible shows "performed" by great actors. Except they were not acting, but losing it. At rehearsals or anywhere away from the audience' eye only. Never in front of an audience. These people, for whom the stage was more than home, who lived on stage, knew its laws and strictly observed them. I am sure that as much as they learned to enact emotion according to the role in a play, they learned early to control their emotions off stage. Even they let everything go sometimes.

I heard a great actor, loved by the whole theatre, go off at a recording studio ranting about something a production manager, a very nice and soft-spoken lady in her late twenties, did or didn't do to his liking. "You don't know who I am!" "Who are you talking to?" She didn't say a word. "How dare you?" "Who do you think you are?" Etc. etc. Valentin kept on screaming on top of his lungs. WOW! I was an absolute novice in the world of adults, years before I heard Art Blakey's famous expression for the first time. But it was very clear to me that Valentin was so wrong, so pathetic, so not himself. Yes, he was the main actor, he was under pressure, the whole production depended on his role being performed right. It was too late for any rehearsals, the tapes and cameras were rolling. A professional actor, with years of experience, everybody's hero and being so unreasonable. Just discharging his built up tension on a helpless lady, I kept thinking. As if the uncontrollable beast of a monster possessed him. There was nothing Valentin could've done to get away from the beast's total domination.

How about the main artistic director at the theatre, (let's call him A.G.) a genius. Every actor in the city would consider his/her luck, fortune, privilege to work under him. Boy, didn't this pillar of the Russian Theatrical School provide some wacky spectacles. For some reason when he was screaming it was always funny. One time at the very last run through of a new play, when everybody was near exhaustion after a long day of rehearsals, stops and starts, criticisms he announced "No stopping. No matter what, we keep on moving till the end of the play. Curtain".

The curtain had just started to slowly move when a loud shriek, piercing the dead silence, announced "That is not how you open the curtain. That is not the way to start the very first act of a play. Start over, immediately. Right this minute". Wild laughter, louder even than the shriek, shook the theatre to its foundation. Everybody burst out laughing: make-up artists, stage hands, delivery men, not to mention all the actors, cleaning ladies, everybody was overtaken by laughter. Another time the artistic director instructed his wife. - "Play this scene exactly the same way as when you sit in front of the mirror and get ready for a night out, God damn it!" What happened was that his wife, a beautiful young lady and the main character in all of the plays in the theater's repertoire, while rehearsing had to go through a scene where her character was in front of a mirror and putting makeup on. Again and again it was nothing convincing. Try again, again, again......... A.G. did control his emotions for a very long time until the "emotion control" muscle got exhausted and he exploded. His wife was hurt. One could see it. No laughter this time either.

Some sound engineers are actually known for not even trying to resist the urge of letting the tension go. It takes as little as a musician touching a piece of studio equipment. The most famous, Hollywood actors and actresses loved by millions, prima donnas, prima ballerinas, painters, etc. Some become addicted to scandal. Unable to live without a scandal, thriving on, looking for, creating a scandal. - Trouble, Trouble..............

Why do we need to control our emotions? - We have already talked about tension. Remember when I talked about breathing? Under tension one can't even talk, let alone play the trumpet. Remember? That's why. Because one person lets it go, explodes, screams and yells, - everybody around him tenses up, freezes, immobilizes. All the mental and physical faculties come to a stand-still, literally. The lecturer is gasping for words, the world's greatest boxer gets knocked out. Yeah, yeah, trash talk in sports is there for a reason. One person at a recording studio messes it up for everybody around him. "The collective product" goes down the drain.

Some club owners, band leaders and great musicians were even worse than the actor I watched at my very first professional gig. It's not that I heard somebody reciting a story or heard it on a tape. No, I was there and witnessed the whole scene. I mean, this is no speculation or retelling somebody else's story, nor exaggerating. Oh, boy! Want me to identify everybody? Here we go.

No, I don't want to spoil it for you and leave you disillusioned. Do keep in mind though

"DON'T MAKE A GOD OUT OF A HUMAN BEING".

Who said it, remember? Art Blakey, of course. Yet, I don't want your hero to fall of the pedestal and crash into pieces. That is not what this book is all about. But I will tell you a story I heard from Art Blakey many times, the story of him playing drums in Duke Ellington's orchestra:

"He (Duke Ellington) was always, at all times, so kind, patient, friendly, considering, respectful, well-wishing, that you would fall under the charm of his personality and watch your own move to the background. That's how strong his influence was. At one point I realized that I had to leave if I wanted to remain myself, to keep my personality, whatever it was."

Art Blakey did leave. At that age, to part with one of the greatest bands in jazz history is a feat of its own! Did you guess yet what would've happened or not happened if Art Blakey clung to the safety of his chair in Duke's band. No? We would've never had Art Blakey & the Jazz Messengers. How about that?!

Of course I heard Art Blakey telling stories of Clifford Brown - My undisputed trumpet hero. "Clifford? - Always soft spoken, never any substances, absolutely clean, never arguing with anybody". This other story I had also heard Art deliver a few times: "Once, at Birdland, we did not get paid after a gig. The joint was being run by mobsters. Nobody had enough balls to walk into their room and demand what was due to us. Nobody, except Clifford, small and quiet young man as he was. He just opened the door, walked in and walked out with the money in his hand, not even losing too much time inside."

For a very long time I thought the story had been a kind of fiction, designed to glorify Clifford. But no. Years after I heard it from Blakey, I read it on the Internet coming from Max Roach. Word for word, exactly the same story. It had to be true then! The subtext, of course, was: If anybody else, some big and burly guy for example, walked into that room full of mafia guys and demanded the money not showing "due respect", he would've been moved out of that room feet first, in no time". What else is there to say? - Control your emotions.

Athletes have to deal with emotions too. As I have mentioned before, musicians and athletes have a lot in common. Just to remind you: Muscle coordination, Timing, Emotion are the most important common denominators. There are prima donnas in sports too. Some do let go off their emotions a lot. Some learn to control the "beast". Have you ever seen a John McEnroe vs. Bjorn Borg match? What a wealth of illustration of this point! I know those Face-Offs are a legend and maybe there is no point retelling a story everybody knows. But I will give you a short synopsis here any way.

When these two tennis giants and adversaries squared off, it was like a battle of two completely opposite worlds - on one side of the court you have a world of strung up nerves ready to pop at any, even remotely, questionable call and on the other a perfect picture of the three C's: Cool, Calm and Collected - no matter what happened, no matter how unfair or wrong a decision the umpire had made, it wouldn't make any difference. The other "world" would appear totally indifferent and no single facial nor otherwise muscle would move to betray a happy or unhappy reaction. Besides the game itself, that contrast alone was worth coming to the stadium and watching, an amazing show.

Of course here we are dealing with two diametrically reverse concepts: the first one - it's much safer to release nervous tension than keep it inside and build up unwanted pressure. The other one: don't let the nerves go off, let them convert into energy and use that energy for something else. To play tennis, for example, or play trumpet, for that matter.

Which concept is correct? I vote for the second one, of course. Besides becoming a nuisance with a nasty personality, not learning to suppress attacks of nerves, anger, jealousy, whatever, one ends up being eaten alive by those monsters. Literally. Have you heard of ulcers, heart attacks, apoplexy etc? From nerves, that's where they come from. The medical community assures us of that. Just like a Russian saying goes - All ailments come from nerves. Only gonorrhea, a sexually transmitted disease, comes from pleasure.

Enough of that. I'd rather hear what Art Blakey had to say about this. Oh sure, of course, here it is: "Control your emotions. Learn to control your emotions". Alright? You heard that? Thank you!

If you still need a second opinion, go ahead and look for one. Not me. This is the first, the last and the only opinion for me. You know why? Because every one of Art's statement I discuss here proved to be true, correct, to the point and valid. Everyone.

"CONTROL YOUR EMOTIONS."

- ART BLAKEY.

We certainly heard it from him more than once.

Etc. Etc. Etc.

"WHAT'S THE NAME OF THAT TUNE?"

Every time he (Art Blakey) heard a tune he learned at the beginning of his musical journey, at the time of his musical infancy, we would necessarily hear this classic. I certainly heard it at Michel's, when blowing on "The Theme Song" I quoted "Lester Leaps In", which is on the same changes, of course, and choked on my own laughter. It was so funny to hear it coming from Art, who was there when Lester Young played it for the first time. Or, who knows, maybe even played it with him. Another time, we had just arrived at a jazz club in Europe somewhere and were warming up before the audience entered. Only Art was sitting down, assuming the appearance of a sleeping man. The club owner just turned the music on. The first sounds out of the speakers were that of Charlie Parker playing Now's The Time. Art Blakey, with his eyes wide open, sat up and in a very firm voice inquired "What's the name of that tune?" Bobby (Watson), who was practicing in the next room, came running in with his Selmer alto sax hanging on his neck, trying to play the classic melody too. But he broke into laughter with the rest of us instead.

"GIVE ME MY MONEY."

This one I heard only once. But it could've not made a stronger impression on me had I heard it a zillion times. I'd better say, the situation occurred only once, at least in my presence. But he kept repeating the phrase and kept raising the volume of his voice again and again, starting from mezzo piano to mf to f, ff, fff etc. until the volume was so unbearably loud that the agent, who Art was talking to and had his money, couldn't take it any more, reached into his pocket, unearthed a rather thick envelope and handed it to its rightful owner. Wasn't that a learning experience!?

I had heard that in the early days of the Soviet Union people were snatched off the streets and driven to the V.Ch.K. - The All-Russian Extraordinary Commission (Future KGB) headquarters to disappear for a long time, if not forever. But, if the victim had a chance to scream on top of his/her lungs, the secret police men in trench coats would set that victim loose and drive away. What a trick! Saving lives just like that? But, where had Art learnt it? Hm!

"DON'T LISTEN TO WHAT PEOPLE SAY, WATCH WHAT THEY DO."

Of course one can experience the wisdom of this saying coming from many different sources, not only from a musical giant. This one I was very familiar with since my childhood. But I heard it many times from Art Blakey too. Many times. I still hear Art's voice in my ears, but do not remember the circumstances. Now I start to think he was commenting on a concrete situation at the moment, I am almost certain now, when somebody had proclaimed something, but did totally the opposite. Was it me? What?! Some thought! No, not possible. Then I would've remembered the scene.

"NO AMERICA - NO JAZZ."

"In Foreign countries the most famous men from our country are Louis Armstrong, Duke Ellington, Benny Goodman, Charlie Parker etc. Jazz Artists. Jazz. They are more famous throughout the world than our presidents".

But, everything comes from another country, one would say. Yes, that's true, but in America, that's where African and European cultures merged and gave birth to an absolutely new form of art. And what an art form at that! Jazz.

Only in America was it possible. No America, No Jazz. This statement of Art Blakey's goes with "Give Credit Where it's Due", too. Yes, it is now all over the world - loved, respected as the greatest art form of the 20th Century, performed, studied, researched, preserved. But it was born in America on the cotton fields, then the rest of America picked it up, then it became so popular everywhere else on the planet that it's now a part of the cultural life of each and every country around the Globe.

Just like the music of the world's greatest classical composers, whether German, Austrian, French or Russian, you name it, Jazz belongs to the whole world now. But it was born and evolved in America. No America, No Jazz.

Right out of that concept comes this next phrase of Art's:

"THEY DO IT (PLAYING JAZZ) IN AFRICA, EUROPE, JAPAN, BRAZIL, IN RUSSIA."

This one was not so much for us in the band but for the American audiences. As for me, coming from Russia, I already knew first hand what an impact jazz had made on the world. It was the same for the rest of the band having traveled all over the world year around. At the Village Gate, the Village Vanguard and other downtown venues patronized by foreign tourists, there was no need to reiterate the idea. But at Michel's, which was always packed by locals, he would very often "open" their eyes to what was taken for granted - Jazz, The greatest artistic creation of 20th Century!

"I GOTTA PLAY PHYSICALLY AND SPIRITUALLY, THE WHOLE GROUP THAT PUTS IT TOGETHER, THIS IS DEMOCRACY, EVERYBODY CAN CONTRIBUTE. MESSED UP YOUR CHOP? YOU GOTTA DANCE, BALLERINA. IT IS A SPIRITUAL MUSIC FROM THE CREATOR TO THE ARTIST. THERE IS NO MUSIC IN THE WORLD LIKE THAT, NONE. SPLIT SECOND TIME AND YOU ARE A PART OF IT. ONCE AN IDEA IS BORN IT DOESN'T BELONG TO THE INDIVIDUAL WHO BRINGS FORTH THE IDEA. THE IDEA BELONGS TO THE WHOLE WORLD"

(ART BLAKEY)

I am sure as soon as I leave these pages and try to do something else, another of Art Blakey's wise sayings will pop up in my mind and then another one. By then I will already be engrossed in something else. What that something else is not too difficult to guess, of course - practicing the trumpet, then writing new arrangement for my Our Father Who Art Blakey Big Band. Then another quote will pop up, no doubt. So, I will be collecting them, of course. Maybe you could send me one I have missed. That'll be great! Thank you in advance! When I amass enough of them, I will take a break from the trumpet, arrangements and get back to writing, this time my ***V.M.Ponomarev's Graduation dissertation volume II.***

It goes without saying, will give you credit too. Give credit where it's due, remember? I hope it won't take too long. In the mean time, please, come to

The Jazz Messengers: The Legacy of Art Blakey led by Valery Ponomarev sextet and *VP's Our Father Who Art Blakey Big Band* concerts, wherever they may take place. We will always be happy to see you and play for you. And we will quote Art Blakey from the stage for you too.

Till then yours truly,
Valery Messenger Ponomarev
7/04/19

ABOUT THE AUTHOR

Short Bio - *Jazz trumpeter Valery Ponomarev* was born in Russia and came to the U.S. in 1973. He has been an American citizen since 1979, and has worked with Art Blakey & the Jazz Messengers for four years. With the Messengers, he performed at major concert halls, clubs, and festivals all over the world and recorded 11 albums. He also made numerous television appearances with the Messengers in Europe, Japan, and Brazil. In the United States, he has made television appearances on "To Tell the Truth," on the PBS network, National Geographic Today, and CNN.

The long list of jazz luminaries Mr. Ponomarev performed, traveled and recorded with, in addition to Art Blakey and The Jazz Messengers, includes super stars of modern jazz such as: Benny Golson, Max Roach, Joe Henderson, Jimmy Cobb, Don Braden, Curtis Fuller, Charles McPherson, Mark Gross, the Duke Ellington Orchestra under Mercer and Paul Ellington, the Arturo O'Farril Afro Cuban Jazz Big Band and many others.

He recorded eight solo albums, most of which originally received the highest ratings . His first book "On the Flip Side of Sound" has generated numerous very favorable comments and reviews by the absolute best in the music business. The 52-minute documentary "Trumpeter from Russia", based on this book, was awarded the Gold Remi Aword at the 2011 Houston, TX International Film Festival. His life is also documented in short films "Messenger from Russia" and "Frozen in Amber".

In addition to playing with his quintet, Mr.Ponomarev leads and writes for his big band VPJBB a.k.a. "Our Father Who Art Blakey". The VPJBB performed at Dizzy's, Iridium, Jazz Standard, and other venues in NYC and appears regularly at the legendary "Zinc Bar" in the Village. The band's CD featuring Benny Golson accumulated numerous glowing and rave reviews. It also made the list of the best recordings of 2016.

Valery Ponomarev Big Band: Our Father Who Art Blakey : The Centennial – Summit Records. Release date January 17/2020. Reviews are being posted on Mr. V.Ponomarev's FaceBook page as they appear in the press.

The most typical comments: **And I give all the credit to Valery for his excellent writing and keeping the Messengers' spirit alive and well.** ...a band to perform large-ensemble versions of Messenger classics .....faithful representations of the source material, more reincarnation than reimagination.

Valery Ponomarev is a hard bop trumpeter who plays with both fire and sensitivity..... has put together first class band that has a solid footing in hard bop jazz.

...the arrangements do not copy the past and instead are creative within the hardbop genre.

...Art Blakey would have enjoyed sitting in with this big band.

For fans of great jazz played right, not just fans of Blakey, this fast ball right down the middle hits all the right notes in fine form.

It is obvious that Mr. Ponomarev knows how to capture the energy and essence of Art Blakey.

...this reviewer's opinion that Valery Ponomarev's big band makes magical music. You will enjoy playing this gutsy, energized, hardbop album over and over again.